The Seven Essentials of
WOODWORKING

The Seven Essentials of
WOODWORKING

Anthony Guidice

Sterling Publishing Co., Inc.
New York

684.08
GUI

Published by Sterling Publishing Company, Inc.
387 Park Avenue South, New York, N.Y. 10016
© 2001 by Anthony Guidice
Distributed in Canada by Sterling Publishing
℅ Canadian Manda Group, One Atlantic Avenue, Suite 105
Toronto, Ontario, Canada M6K 3E7
Distributed in Great Britain and Europe by Cassell PLC
Wellington House, 125 Strand, London WC2R 0BB, England
Distributed in Australia by Capricorn Link (Australia) Pty, Ltd.
P.O. Box 704, Windsor, NSW 2756 Australia
Printed in China
All rights reserved
Sterling ISBN 0-8069-2527-2
3   5   7   9   10   8   6   4   2

Drawings by Anthony Guidice
Photography by Vicki Guidice

A Note to the Reader:

Working wood is potentially dangerous. Using hand or power tools or neglecting safety prac-tices can lead to injury. Don't perform any operations learned here until you are certain they can be performed safely.

The author and editor have tried to make all information as accurate as possible. How-ever, due to the construction materials, skill level of the reader, and other factors, neither the author nor Sterling Publishing assumes any responsibility for injuries or damages.

This book is for
Vicki & for Sarah

Contents

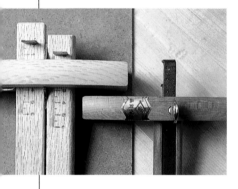

Five

USING HAND PLANES

Six

MAKING MORTISE & TENON JOINTS

Seven

WOOD FINISHING

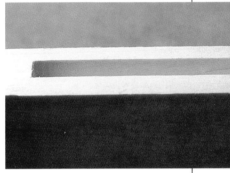

APPENDICES

THE ESSENTIAL INTRODUCTION

"The stuff we see in class is all supposed to be good. The books show work that's good, and all the music on the classical station is good. It would really help to see what isn't good."

—Rochester Institute of Technology graduate student, 1979, discussing art and aesthetics

I once knew of a woodworking shop in Florissant, Missouri. The owners had an idea that if they hired unskilled workers to make things only with machinery, they could turn out good work. Then they could pay the workers low wages and make an easy profit. The shop turned out lousy work and the clients didn't want to pay for it, and the owners were out of business in a year and a half.

What does this mean—that woodworking machines do lousy work? No.

Some time after this, I traveled to California, to do a magazine article at a woodworking school there. Students prided themselves on learning the teachings of the "Master," taking days and sometimes weeks to do the simplest things by hand. "How long does it take you to cut these dovetails?" I would ask. "Two weeks," was the answer. The continuous lament from these students and their teacher was that the public didn't want to pay the high prices for the questionable work being produced.

What does this mean—that hand-tool work is no good? Of course not.

Both are examples of extreme approaches to woodworking. Too much emphasis on machine work can dull your sensitivity. You become a machine operator. Doing handwork with the wrong tools and methods is slow and frustrating. Either way, you'll achieve fine work only by accident, and only occasionally.

What's the best approach? That's where you understand the way wood behaves (pretty simple) and the logical way to put it together (make joints). That's about it for wood. The other thing you need to know is what tools to use to work the wood and how to use them.

Isn't this what all woodworking books describe? Yes. Then why do you need this one?

The following pages present the format of a basic woodworking course I teach. In it, the students are required to master fundamental hand-tool skills and principles—measuring and marking boards, sawing to a line, sharpening blades, using planes, etc.—before being allowed to operate machines. These are skills that, once you know them thoroughly, allow you to deal with virtually any woodworking situation. This is quite different from most woodworking books, which hurl thousands of methods at you, insisting that you learn every one, and maybe, when you're presented with a problem, the answer should be in there somewhere.

Ridiculous.

This book covers hand-tool methods, but it isn't just about woodworking by hand. There are no woodworking machines discussed here except a grinder, but that doesn't make it a statement against woodworking machines (I own lots of woodworking machines—couldn't make a living without them). This book discusses a *philosophy*. Once you understand this philosophy, it won't matter if you make art furniture or birdhouses, or whether you use hand tools or machines. Your approach to your work will be sound and you will be able to solve whatever woodworking problem you may come across, even if you've never done it before. Examples: If you know what makes an optimum glue joint, you'll be able to make one using any method (**I–1**). If you know how a properly set and sharpened saw blade should work (**I–2**), you'll know when one *isn't* working—whether it's a table-saw, band-saw, or handsaw blade. If you know when a board is "flat" because you've learned how to flat-

I–2. ◆ *A close-up of the teeth on a bow saw showing the proper amount of set. Chapter Four discusses sharpening techniques for bow saws, plane irons, chisels, etc.*

ten one, you'll always know when boards are flat—whether you flatten them by hand or with machines.

WHAT WORKS, WORKS

Whenever I write a magazine article about hand woodworking, I always get letters from people who want to argue, among other things, the relative merits of using saws different than the ones I use; of scouring antique tool shows instead of just buying a good tool to start with; and of endlessly fiddling with inferior hand planes to get them to work rather than simply using a good-quality one. These people are more interested in tinkering and puttering (and arguing) than they are with finding out what works and doing it. My methods aren't the only ones out there, and they are not even the only ones that work. But they do work, and are the fastest. In my workshops, if students do just what I tell them, and use

I–1. ◆ *This mortise-and-tenon joint is an excellent glue joint because of the long-grain surfaces in the mortises (holes) and the tenons (projecting pieces). Chapter One discusses optimum glue joints, and Chapter Six discusses how to make mortise-and-tenon joints.*

the tools I tell them to use, they can achieve results easier and faster than any other way.

You'd be amazed how many known "experts" I've spoken to who have never used a scrub plane, don't know what the proper "set" on a handsaw is, or even what a *good* handsaw is. They can cut their way through miles of wood with machinery, but none of them can tell you the true value of a well-made mortise-and-tenon joint ("it holds two pieces of wood together" is not the answer) or how to *correctly* surface a board by hand. Amazing.

Then there are the honest-to-goodness, true experts. I've known some of them—people who have studied in Germany, Denmark, and Hungary as apprentices. Although they all use machines, they can also perform any woodworking task with hand tools if need be. They know they can't make a good shaving with some new planes; that the standard carpenter's handsaw (a panel saw) doesn't cut well; and that most modern chisels get dull so fast they're not worth using. They learned the right way once and stuck to it for a lifetime, never becoming caught up in the endless experimentation that many woodworkers spend years on. It's amazing that some folks, who can use all the help they can get, spend much of their time struggling with questionable tools and methods that the European-trained woodworkers would never *consider* using, and then argue about them! They are like abstract painters who can't draw.

Within these pages are the first things you should know about working with wood. It's one thing to know the fundamentals and

then choose to use machines for professional or production reasons; but most woodworkers don't have sound hand-tool skills. They use machines because it's easy to use machines and because they can't use hand tools properly, not because they choose not to. Proper handwork gives you the foundation on which all else is based. And some problems can't be solved with machines.

This book describes some specific methods and procedures that will obtain a noticeable improvement in your woodworking awareness and skills. Because the right tools solve about 80 to 90 percent of hand-tool problems, some specific tools are mentioned and required for best results. The techniques described will be frustrating if alternate tools are substituted, or if you use a shortcut. You can't make a good omelette with rotten eggs, and you can't do precision handwork with poor tools.

I am very much aware that some of the precepts in this book are contrary to what is often written in woodworking books and magazines, and may be challenged by "experts." Because I use these techniques and principles every day in my shop, I can say assuredly that they represent what actually does happen in working with wood—not what should happen, might happen, or will theoretically happen.

The confusing, overcomplicated format of most woodworking books has been avoided here; at times the text may seem to leave some questions unanswered. I find it best to cover the main points first and pick up the loose ends later. There are repetitions, intentionally stated, that are integral to the effectiveness of the book.

Do you want to be a top-notch woodworker? It's simple (but not easy). Pay attention to the information in the following pages. Then buy a quality handsaw and learn to crosscut and rip hardwood boards by hand. Good. Now learn to edge-joint and surface a three-foot plank by hand. Then see if you can sharpen tools better, sharper, and faster than anyone. Finally, cut a mortise-and-tenon joint by hand and become completely familiar with one finishing technique. Do that and you'll have no competition. That's what's in the book.

Anthony Guidice

1–3. ◆ *Author Anthony Guidice in his workshop.*

PREAMBLE:
SOME NOTES ON BEING A WOODWORKER

Being a practitioner of any discipline—whether woodworking, painting, music, writing, etc.—requires a certain amount of commitment. That means investing part of your life in this discipline, and it also means hard work. You can't just buy a violin or a guitar and become a musician. Similarly, owning a table saw and some power tools doesn't necessarily make you a woodworker, either. The study and mastery of the skills make you a woodworker. That study involves learning to think properly as well as doing the actual work.

Many students have wrong ideas about the tools, the material, and the correct approach for woodworking. They aren't thinking properly at the start. After all, some things are possible—and reasonable to expect—and some simply aren't. The correct mindset at the start is of primary importance.

THE WORKSHOP

A comfortable shop (1) is a necessity for serious work. My shop is pretty small. It's in a reconverted 1910 carriage house. My last shop was even smaller than that—the wood rack shared space with the laundry room. Even so, I did lots of good work in there, and made a lot of money, too. It wasn't very big, but it had what is essential for a good shop. I'll mention a few shop tips here.

A shop should have good lighting. I have six double fluorescent fixtures for general

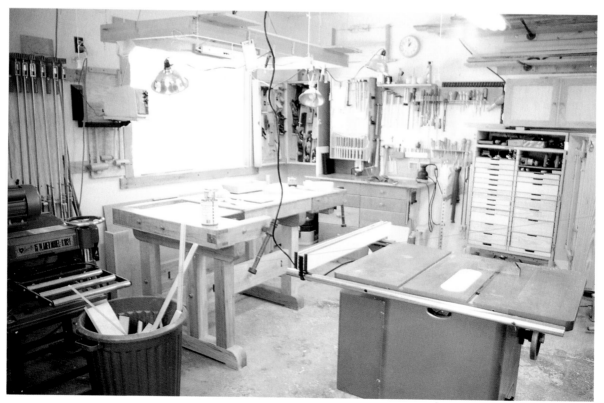

1. ◆ *The author's workshop.*

room lighting and individually clamped lights with tungsten bulbs and reflectors over the workbench. If you're going to mark accurately within the width of a knife line, you have to see the workpiece to mark it. It isn't necessary that all the lights be on all the time, but where you are working, good light is a must—especially around any machines.

Make sure the shop is always tidy. I like to remove everything from the countertops and the tool tray on my bench and put these items away until I'm ready to use them again. This is especially true for small shops. No one can work well with piles of tools and scrap wood lying around everywhere. At the workbench, only one workpiece should be on the surface at a time. If I have four table legs that will be worked on, I work on one and put the other three on the roll-around cart or on the countertop next to me.

It is especially important to keep the floor tidy. Sweep it frequently and keep it clean so you always have good footing, whatever you're doing. I don't need to tell you what can happen if you lose your footing around a spinning table-saw blade. Some folks tell me they're too busy to keep their own shops tidy all the time. Nonsense. I do plenty of work—personal and professional—and my shop is always neat and clean.

Make sure you have a good vise to hold the work. It doesn't matter if you use a Scandinavian bench like the one I use (2) or an

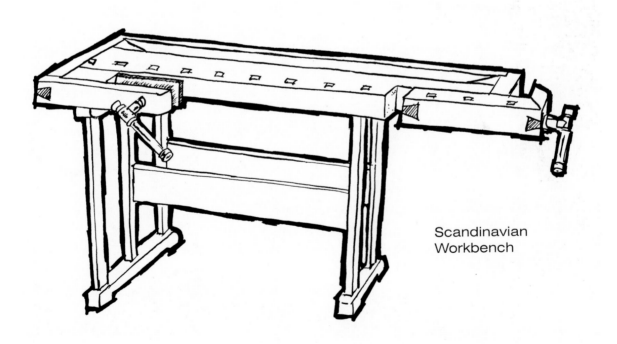

Scandinavian
Workbench

2. ◆ *Scandinavian-style workbench. This bench allows the most efficient ways to hold wood for planing, joinery, etc. Luxurious, but not indispensable.*

English-style workbench with an iron vise on it (3), but it's important that the work is held firmly while you saw, chisel, and mark it. Otherwise, woodworking can not only be dangerous, but thoroughly frustrating. Wendell Castle, the art furnituremaker, uses a hydraulically controlled bench with a pattern-maker's vise on it. Arthur Chapin uses an ancient iron vise on an equally ancient workbench. Both work.

Some additional safety tips: When you chisel, keep the other hand behind the blade. When you saw, keep the other hand where the saw won't cut it if it jumps out of the kerf. (Don't laugh. I once had to go to the hospital because of a cut from a 9-point bow saw blade, a *handsaw*! I left the blood spots on the floor as a reminder.) Don't shortcut any steps when working around machines, and know all your machines intimately before you use them. Don't ever rush. A good craftsman never rushes. Never work when you are tired or run down physically for any reason (or taking cold medication). Concentrate. Always concentrate. Don't get distracted while attempting to do any work. Remove the distraction or stop working. Use good tools and don't lend your tools to friends. You don't want to lose your tools or your friends.

WOOD: BEAUTIFUL, NATURAL, INEXACT

Wood is in a constant state of flux. It moves, twists, cracks, warps, and bends. It's also a

English-Style Woodworking Vise

3. ◆ *An English-style woodworking vise like this one can be outfitted to any type of workbench and is perfectly adequate for holding wood while you work it.*

pretty easy material to work with, so usually those problems can be resolved. It's a mistake, however, to ever assume that the characteristics of wood are absolute. I hear terms thrown around all the time about wood: "perfectly square," "perfectly straight," etc. Sorry, but this is not so. Nothing about wood is absolute. You'll never get a board "perfectly" anything. If I flatten a board in my shop, leave it on the bench, and it rains overnight, the next day the board won't be as flat anymore. It'll be almost as flat, usably flat, *reasonably* flat, but it won't be as flat as it was. And that's just in one night.

Sometimes boards of the same species of wood cut from the same woodpile will behave unpredictably. I made a Shaker-type utility chest out of northern Missouri hickory for some photographs for the Rhode Island School of Design. (If you're a beginner, don't use hickory until you've got some experience and confidence; it's about as hard as, and works about as easily as, a block of stone.) The chest had a top, sides, drawer frames, and two drawers—a simple design. I made allowances for wood movement on both sides of the chest. The side panels were made from similar boards, from the same tree, dried the same way in the same pile. One side is split and the other isn't.

"Reasonably" is a wonderful word to apply to wood. You can make beautiful furniture with wood that's reasonably flat. It's reasonable to expect some degree of tear-out when you plane a board. A carcass or large drawer box, for example, should be reasonably square—within about 1/32 of an inch. That's fine. It's unnecessary to get it any closer. So have reasonable expectations of how wood behaves. It never will be "perfectly" anything ... except beautiful.

Wood—whether it is still part of the tree or in board form—is exquisite. Split open a log and you'll see that the grain pattern is magnificent. Lots of woodworkers do horrible things to this material. They stain it, bleach it, plasticize it, fume it—in short, try to make it look like something it's not. Wood gets overfinished, overpolished, overstained, oversanded—overworked. This is not necessary. Smooth it with a plane, or sand it lightly and then oil it. That's enough.

CREATIVITY, DESIGN, PROPORTION

It is important that you learn a good set of woodworking techniques you can use for a lifetime and which will allow you to master the tricky stuff later. This can be done efficiently and quickly through plain hard work. Master these techniques so they become second nature and you are free to concentrate your creative juices on making furniture and other woodworking projects that are well-proportioned, pleasing to look at, and useful.

Most students get this backward. They grab a set of plans from a book or magazine for something to make—a table, a chest ... whatever. They leave all the creative work for a moment's thought, dependent on someone else's design. Then when they get to building it, every step is a new adventure (or worse, a new gamble). What should be quick and repeatable—like flattening boards, edge-jointing, sharpening—becomes an act of meditation. Slow meditation. Not good.

Please don't misunderstand. When fitting drawers, assembling a complicated carcass, or doing final surfacing, you need to take your time and get it right—as exact as the material will let you. The same holds true when you're designing something—you need to get the proportions right. Properly proportioned parts make the furniture look good (**4** and **5**). This takes time. You don't want the piece heavy and horsey-looking, nor so fragile-looking that it appears a slight wind might knock it down. But the mechanical operations should be done as quickly and repetitively as possible.

There are a lot of these mechanical, repetitive operations in woodworking, from sawing a straight line to getting a razor-sharp edge on a tool quickly. I was at a woodworking school one time where students were nearing the end of a three-month course. I

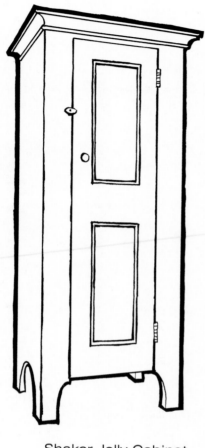

Shaker Jelly Cabinet

4. ◆ A Shaker jelly cabinet with a misleadingly simple design. It's very tough to design and make things that look like this. If any of the proportions or shapes in this piece were wrong, it wouldn't look good.

watched one student cut the end off a board. He marked it, clamped it to the bench, and then cut it, rotating and clamping it as he was cutting. Something that should have taken 30 to 40 seconds took him about 10 minutes. That's too much time.

Why is learning the proper woodworking technique so important? Woodworking is already by its very nature time-consuming. Things often take twice as long to do as you initially think they will (ask any professional in a small shop). You really can't afford to be spending over a half hour making four cuts that should take less than three minutes. It's too inefficient. If you're a pro, you'll go broke. If you're a hobbyist, you already have limited time. Why waste it? Also, there is a

5. ◆ A Shaker chest of drawers. What's so difficult about making a chest with four drawers in it? Plenty! What this is, is a series of rectangles that are so well proportioned it becomes something more than furniture. And you can still sweep underneath it.

Shaker Chest of Drawers

limited amount of time in the workshop in which you can work at peak efficiency. Save it for difficult tasks, like cutting a sliding dovetail joint* (6), which is important for carcass construction, or shaping a precise curve or detail. Don't waste energy and brainpower on rudimentary things like gluing up panels or sharpening chisels. This is also why I don't make my own tools, fix up antique ones, or even tune up new tools that aren't precisely made. I want to wisely spend all of my valuable (and limited) time and energy on woodworking—making the stuff.

*This joint, which is not covered in this book, requires precise use and control of woodworking tools, topics that are covered.

So proper, rigorous, efficient technique is a totally practical idea. It frees you up to spend the correct amount of time on woodworking tasks that require extra care, and for designing and thinking the piece through. It simply allows you to use your personal resources better.

JOINERY FACTS AND MYTHS

Making strong, functional woodworking joinery depends on two things: knowing which joint to use and how to make it. Whether you're making a lapped gooseneck mortise-and-tenon joint (*mechigai-koshikake-kama-tsugi*) for a Japanese temple beam (7)

Sliding Dovetail Joint

6. ◆ *The sliding dovetail joint. This important joint allows a firm connection, yet still permits wood movement. I've met two people in my life who could make one by hand.*

7. ◆ *A Japanese lapped-gooseneck mortise-and-tenon joint. Japanese woodworkers have such magnificent control of their tools they can mark out and cut a joint like this in an amazingly short time.*

Mechigai-Koshikake-Kama-Tsugi

or a nailed butt joint for a birdhouse (**8**), these two things always apply. The key to making a variety of joints is to know how to make *one* joint—the essential or "core" joint. Then you can figure out how to make any other one—*provided you have the ability to control the correct tools properly.* (Even a nailed butt joint needs two straight sides to "butt" together, so if you can't control a plane and a saw, you can't even make that.)

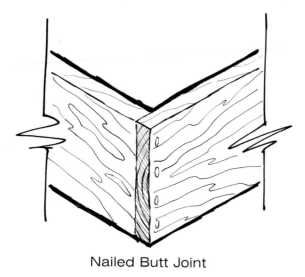

Nailed Butt Joint

8. ◆ *A nailed butt joint—the easiest-to-make joint, but usually a poor choice for any quality project. Still, if you can't saw and plane the end-grain piece, and plane the long-grain edge accurately, you won't be able to make even this.*

9. ◆ *Carcass construction is used in cabinets, furniture casework, boxes, etc. Frame construction is used in doors, picture frames, and cabinet face frames. Each type of construction uses joinery specific to it.*

There are lots of joints—hundreds of them. Some are "carcass" joints and some are "frame" joints (**9**). Carcass joints are used in cabinets, furniture casework, boxes, etc. Frame joints are used in doors, picture frames, and cabinet face frames. Some "experts" try to teach you all of them at once!

Dovetail joints (**10**) are used in drawers and cabinet casework, as are box joints (**11**). A box joint is a straight dovetail joint, best made by machine. Tongue-and-groove (**12**) and rabbet joints (**13**) are two carcass joints. Spline joints can be for either frame or carcass construction. The machined biscuit joint (**14**)—which consists of compressed wood wafers inserted into slots cut by a biscuit jointer—is a spline joint.

A sliding dovetail joint, as shown in **6**, is a very important joint that is used to hold wide carcasses together without bowing, but

Carcass-and-Frame Construction

Carcass

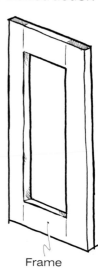

Frame

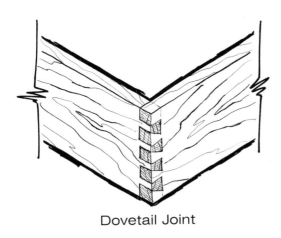

Dovetail Joint

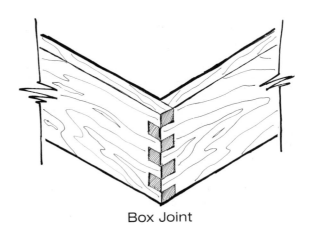

Box Joint

10. ◆ *A "through" dovetail joint. One of the most popular and visible woodworking joints, it has lots of glue surface and great mechanical strength. For small quantities, this joint is best made by hand.*

11. ◆ *A box joint. "Fingers" interlock each other, allowing lots of glue surface. It is easy and fast to make by machine.*

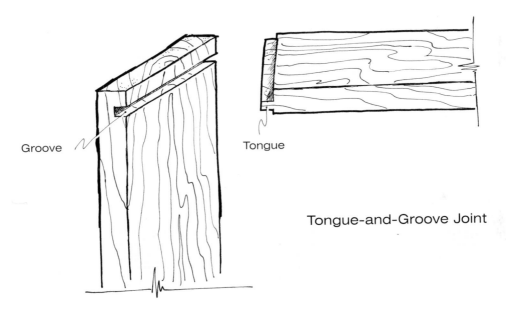

Groove

Tongue

Tongue-and-Groove Joint

12. ◆ *A tongue-and-groove joint used in carcass construction. It is a somewhat poor joint for a carcass, having no glue surface and minimal mechanical strength.*

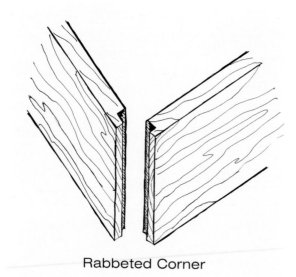

Rabbeted Corner

13. ◆ *A rabbeted corner joint, also shown in carcass construction. This joint also has no glue surface and minimal mechanical strength. It's better than a nailed butt joint, but not much.*

14. ◆ *The biscuit joint—a "high-tech" spline joint. Prefabricated, compressed "biscuits" fit into slots cut with a dedicated machine. It is remarkably strong and useful.*

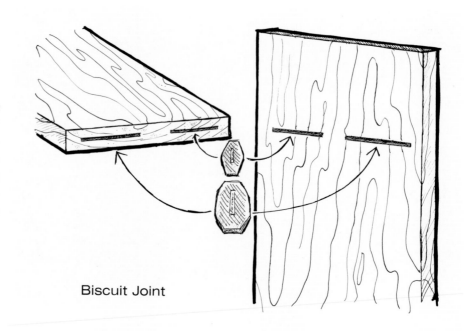

Biscuit Joint

still permits wood movement. A splined miter joint is stronger than a straight miter joint (15), and a lapped miter or mitered bridle joint (16) is even stronger than the splined version, but more difficult to clamp (sometimes you may not need the strength of those joints, and a straight miter is fine).

These are just a few joints that are possible. Confused? Don't fret. You do not need to know them all. Certainly not now.

The keys to successful joint-making are marking the boards correctly, controlling the tools, and using a consistent, simplified approach. Most methods you'll read about in

15. ◆ "Straight" and "splined" miter joints. The spline adds glue surface to the joint and makes it stronger. The straight version is little more than an end-grain joint.

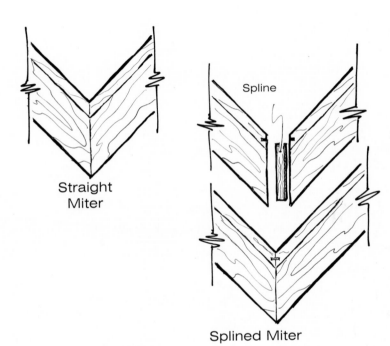

Straight Miter

Spline

Splined Miter

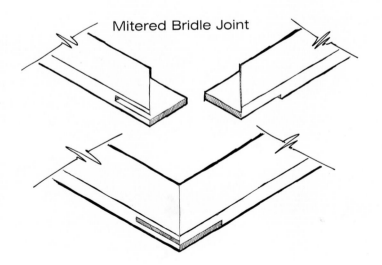

Mitered Bridle Joint

16. ◆ The mitered bridle joint. It is a wonderfully strong and good-looking joint, almost never seen anymore, but it's also fun to make by hand. It has lots of glue surface and mechanical strength.

magazines or books or see on television don't cover this very well (especially when handsaws are used). The reason students and beginning woodworkers have so much trouble doing handwork of any kind is almost always due to the tools. In book after book, backsaws are recommended for bench sawing, that is, close, accurate sawing. Backsaws (**17**) are heavy, difficult to balance, and unwieldy. All the ones I've seen have teeth that are too small and that are sharpened and set incorrectly. It's difficult to reset and resharpen the tiny teeth, and if it's not done just right, the saw stalls and jerks in the cut. And it doesn't cut well, either. It's slow-too slow. It's at least twice as slow as a bow saw, which is the saw I recommend. (The backsaw does not have the worst saw design I've ever seen; the standard carpenter's handsaw, as shown in **18**, has a thicker blade and bigger teeth, whips and kinks in the cut, and cuts even more slowly.)

So the proper handsaw will solve many of the sawing problems in good joint-making.

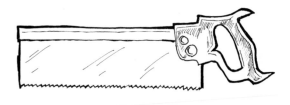

English Backsaw or "Tenon" Saw

17. ◆ *The backsaw, also called a tenon saw. Ubiquitous in woodworking literature, this saw is inefficient and uncomfortable to use. Why have you never heard this before? I don't know.*

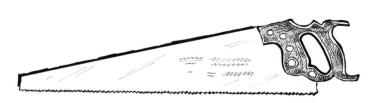

"Standard" Carpenter's Handsaw

18. ◆ *The standard carpenter's handsaw, or panel saw. Older models of this saw cut better than the new ones. That's not saying much. A kitchen bread knife would probably cut better.*

Here's another factor: knowing what a good "fit" is. The correct fit for a woodworking joint is largely a matter of "feel." It has to be. It isn't a constant; it depends on the wood you're using. A good fit in hard maple is different from a good fit in fir or mahogany.

So if all woods respond differently to being sawn, bored, and chiseled, and if the fit of the joint varies depending on what wood you are using, it's best to learn to make only one joint first in one type of wood, and practice making it until you are thoroughly familiar with it. Then you can notice the differences when you make that joint in other types of wood. When you know how one wood behaves, you have a basis for comparison.

USING YOUR WORKSHOP TIME WISELY

I am assuming, throughout this text, that the objective of the woodworker reading it is to make beautiful things from wood. The point of this book is to teach you techniques that can be used permanently so that you can achieve this goal. How much better it is to achieve a solid result instead of going around in circles. Too many woodworkers tinker and experiment with tools trying to get them to work (which is sometimes like trying to raise the dead) and avoid applying their skills in the real world.

I once saw in a catalog of woodworking courses a weeklong class on tuning hand planes. This is silly. Getting a poor hand plane to work as well as it can should take about an hour, more or less, not a week. A plane like that will usually make one type of shaving, at one setting, in one type of situation. Example: It will make a medium-thickness shaving, with the frog set back and the cap iron back, on medium-density hardwoods with not-too-difficult grain.

You can work with planes like this, but it's sort of like driving a car with the emergency brake on. You're handicapped. The better idea is to buy a quality hand plane to start with and then spend time using it to make things. Lots of woodworkers don't like that idea. One wrote to me to complain that the planes I suggested he buy were expensive ($900 for a scrub plane, a low-angle jack plane, and a jointer plane—all of them the finest made). Are they expensive? If you buy a good hand plane, you're assured of a dependable tool. How much does it cost, in terms of time and money, to spend a week tuning an inferior tool? And even then it still won't perform as well as a good one.

What we need to spend a week on is how to make things look good. For example, there should be more classes and books on furniture aesthetics. Why don't we spend hours making sketches of a piece such as a chest of drawers until we have the look just right? Why do we simply follow plans in magazines blindly, never stopping to think, for example, that "that rail looks a little too thick and heavy," or "those drawers are a bit too shallow for clothing," or "how do I improve the look and the usefulness of this piece?" Why do we gloss over the really difficult aspects of woodworking—the areas that the Shakers were so expert at (the proportions of furniture components and the usefulness of the piece), the areas that really take time and study to master (**19**)—and instead spend a week learning how to tune hand planes?

Here's why: because it's easy to tune hand planes and to play around with them. It doesn't take much risk, thought, or study. If you aren't successful, it doesn't really matter much. And there's nothing really wrong with it—you're not hurting anyone, and if you have the time, fine. But the fact remains that this is a way to avoid the real issue. You can become expert at "tuning" every plane on Earth and never make anything worth a damn. Besides, if you use the best tools to begin with, you'll learn all you need to know about hand planes anyway.

TRUST YOURSELF

Let's raise the standards in woodworking, both in technique and aesthetics. This book serves as groundwork for the technique part. I'm more tired than I thought I could be of magazine articles and books that dumb down the woodworking process to make it easy.

Shaker Drop-Leaf Table

19. ◆ A Shaker drop-leaf table—another masterpiece. It is a simple table with a drawer and rear drop leaf. If you can design something like this, you're doing very well. Spend your time studying this kind of woodworking, not experimenting with futile techniques.

Great work in any medium doesn't come from a desire to make things easy. It comes from hard work, a concerted effort to be truly excellent at something.

You already know more than you think you do. Want to make furniture? Well, you've been using furniture all your life. What do you like about it? What don't you like about it? What features in your desk or bedroom chest of drawers, for example, would you like to improve? What types of wood do you prefer? Do you really like walnut because the guy in the woodworking magazine likes it, or do you like something else better? Ever see a piece made from tulipwood (poplar) and finished with linseed oil? It's pretty. How about finishes? Do you like the look of embalmed, plasticized wood? That's what polyurethane does, but the magazine and television guys say you should use it. What do you think? It's completely up to you what design and finish your furniture

has. You probably have some very good ideas but don't trust your judgment.

Here's an idea: Go on a tour of a cheap furniture store! I grew up in a house full of ugly furniture—that ghastly, cheap, production-line stuff made of poplar stained to look like too-bright cherry, and then varnished or lacquered to look like it had been dipped in liquid glass. Design-wise, this furniture was equally awful. It had a smattering of watered-down period details, with equally bad-looking hardware that was much too fancy for the piece. It was difficult to tell what was worse—the design or the finish. I didn't know what I preferred in furniture back then, but it certainly wasn't that.

Then, many years later I saw a Shaker sewing table with drawers, in oiled cherry wood. The wood looked real, touchable, and the oil finish looked pleasant and natural. Similarly, the design was utterly simple and utilitarian, but stunning. Finally here was furniture design that left the wood alone to show its beauty (20). That table was a revelation. I've never gotten over it.

So trust yourself and strive for a higher standard than the pap in most woodworking magazines. Why bother? Because woodworking should be a fine craft in this country. We want to have nice things around us made by people who have an understanding, sensitivity, and conviction about what they're doing (and who are very well paid!). All woodworkers, professional or not, should have a true, in-depth knowledge of the craft rather than a superficial smattering of notions.

Shaker Sewing Table

20. ◆ *Shaker sewing table. This is very similar to the Shaker table I once saw with the beautiful oil finish. With Shaker work like this, the design always fits the material perfectly—the form fits the content. There is never any need to embellish things made of wood.*

WOOD, GLUE SURFACE, & JOINT-MAKING

"What we do not understand, we cannot control."

—**Charles Reich***, *The Greening of America*

Since wood is the indispensable material for everything woodworkers make, we will first discuss some of its characteristics and the way it behaves.

Making strong joints for all types of woodworking project is never a problem if the following is understood:

◆ **1.** An optimum glue joint is one that allows a maximum of *long-grain-to-long-grain glue surface*, as well as a maximum of *mechanical strength*.

◆ **2.** End grain is not a glue surface.**

These rules must be followed to some extent when making all woodworking joints if a good, solid connection is to result. In some cases, the glue surface will predominate, and in others the mechanical strength will, but both must be present to some extent.***

LONG GRAIN AS A GLUE SURFACE

In all woods, the long-grain surfaces will allow glue to adhere and bond the board to

long grain in another board—whether it is on the edge or the face (**1–1 to 1–3**). Long grain will always glue to long grain. This is true for any board, with any glue, in every situation.

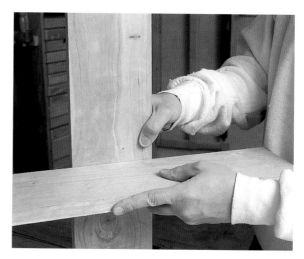

1–1. ◆ *Good glue surface. An edge surface being bonded to a face surface.*

1–2. ◆ *Good glue surface. A face-to-face bonding.*

*Charles Reich is a former Yale Law School Professor and founding board member of the Natural Resources Defense Council.

**It is possible to seal end grain with modern glues and achieve some bonding power to long grain with tight clamping, but this is impractical for most woodworking applications.

*** Some woodworking joints, such as the wedged mortise-and-tenon, etc., are "knock-down" joints that rely completely on mechanical strength and use no glue.

1–3. ◆ *Good glue surface. An edge-to-edge bonding.*

1–4. ◆ *End grain to long grain. Glue will not bond these surfaces, because there is no glue surface.*

End grain is the cut-off end surface of the wood fibers. End grain will not glue to any other surface—whether it is long grain or other end grain (**1–4**). It can be dismissed for use as a working glue surface, and hence ignored when laying out joints or deciding on a joint for any particular project.

It is worthwhile to note that end grain occurs not just on the ends of boards, but in the middle of them as well. As shown in B of **1-5**, the cut section in the board (mortise) is predominately end grain. If we were to cut a piece to fit it (a tenon), the joint would be predominately end grain and wouldn't be very

1–5. ◆ *End grain occurs not just on the ends of boards (as shown in A), but in the middle of boards as well.*

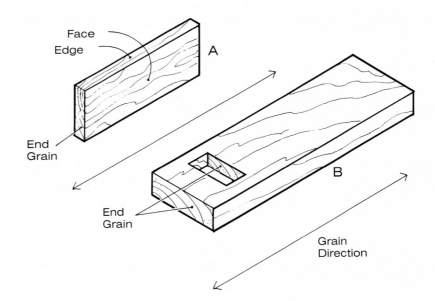

strong (**1–6**). By contrast, **1–7** shows the mortise and tenons cut so as to reveal more long grain, and thus maximize glue surface; this is a much stronger, and thus better, glue joint.

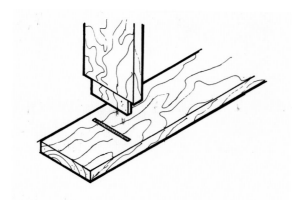

1–6. ◆ *This would be a poor joint because there is almost no glue surface.*

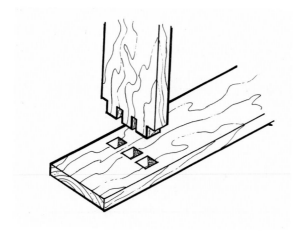

1–7. ◆ *This joint is much better than the joint shown in 1-6 because of the long-grain surfaces in the mortises (holes) and the tenons (projecting pieces).*

Also worth noting is the fact that wood moves. In humid seasons, as it absorbs moisture it expands slightly across the grain; in dry conditions (indoors in winter) it shrinks (**1–8**). In any joint where cross-grain parts are to be glued, this usually isn't

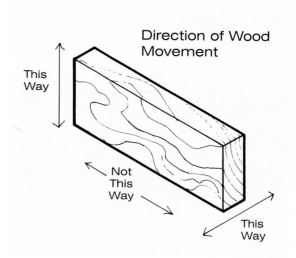

1–8. ◆ *Direction of wood movement.*

a problem if the pieces are about four inches or smaller.

Furniture is a combination of many parts that extend in different directions and at different angles. How can we always get an optimum long-grain-to-long-grain glue surface in all the parts? We can't. We can, however, make the pieces *mechanically strong.*

MECHANICAL STRENGTH

Mechanical strength is simply using the force of one piece of wood against another to resist motion. A nailed butt joint (**1–9**) is a mechanical connection. It isn't a very good one because if you apply even slight pressure to the corner, the joint will loosen. A box made this way will come out of square on all four corners. This is called *racking* (**1–10**). We cannot reinforce this joint with glue because there are no glue surfaces. The only connected parts are end grain to long grain.

1–9. ◆ *The common nailed butt joint is very poor because it has no mechanical strength.*

1–10. ◆ *Any force on the nailed butt joint will cause it to rack, that is, to move.*

In **1–11**, the boards are glued together long grain to long grain—a maximum amount of glue surface. If we notch them as in B, there is still a maximum amount of glue surface (long grain to long grain), but we now have an even better joint because it has mechanical strength, too. This joint is called a *half lap*.

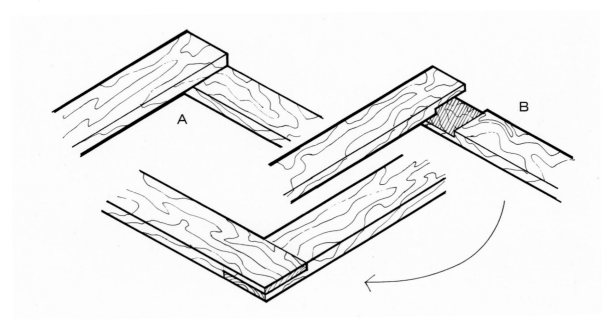

1–11. ◆ *A joint that consists of two boards that have been glued and overlapped (A) has glue surface, but notching it into a half-lap joint (B) now gives it mechanical strength.*

The notched *shoulder* of each piece in the half-lap joint (**1–12**) gives the connection its needed mechanical strength. The force of each shoulder against the other board prevents it from moving. The combination of this mechanical strength plus the maximum long-grain-to-long-grain glue surface makes this half lap a very strong joint. The force required to break it apart would be considerable.

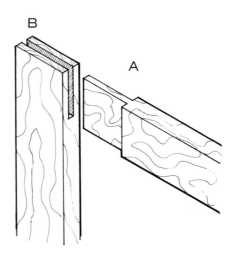

1–13. ◆ *The bridle joint is an optimum woodworking joint because it combines two shoulders and four glue surfaces.*

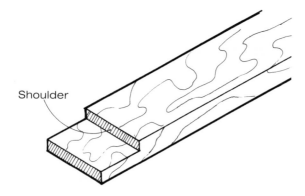

1–12. ◆ *The shoulder of the half-lap joint gives mechanical strength, preventing movement (racking).*

One of my favorite joints is the *bridle joint* (**1–13**). It has two shoulders like the half lap and twice as much glue surface. It is actually an open mortise-and-tenon joint; as shown in **1–13**, piece A has the tenon, and piece B the mortise. We will cut this joint in Chapter Six, both as an open mortise-and-tenon joint and housed. Generally speaking, the mortise-and-tenon joint is the basis for all woodworking joints because it possesses the maximum amount of glue surface with great mechanical strength.

Should the bridle joint always be used in place of the half lap? No, not always. Sometimes you don't need it, as shown in **1–14**.

1–14. ◆ *A half-lap joint used in a cabinet face frame. The face frame is screwed to the cabinet; therefore, the glue surface and mechanical strength of the half-lap joint are perfectly adequate.*

Sometimes the nailed butt joint, as inadequate as it seems, is the right joint to use.

There are many types of woodworking joints because, for example, a small jewelry box won't require the same strength as a chair. The important point is this: Once you can make a good mortise-and-tenon joint, you can make any other joint. Experience will tell you which is the best joint for a given project (1–15). No one single answer will solve all the problems. The same principal—the essential principal—to joint-making will always apply: Maximize glue surface and mechanical strength.

1–15. ◆ *Bridle joint shown in a cabinet door. In this frame-and-panel door, the door stands alone and is hinged to the cabinet. The stronger bridle joint (or open mortise-and-tenon) is a better choice than the half lap.*

GLUE

What is the best glue to use to join joint members? PVA (polyvinyl acetate) glues (1–16) are fine. There are all sorts of confusing marketing terms and buzzwords used to describe PVA glue. White and yellow glues are PVA glue. Carpenter's yellow glue is a bit thicker than white glue, dries faster, and sands better, so it is a good glue to use. All PVA glues clean up with water, and are nontoxic, inexpensive, and more than strong enough for use on anything.

1–16. ◆ *White and yellow woodworking glues. All are PVA (polyvinyl acetate) adhesives and will work well. What's important is to use one exclusively for a while and learn its characteristics.*

A good long-grain-to-long-grain glue bond will be stronger than the actual wood. If you break two well-glued boards joined this way, they will always break in a spot other than the glue joint. When glue manufacturers say their glue forms a bond stronger than the wood itself, this is true. But it is also true of all glues used for wood. Ignore the marketing slogans. Just choose one good yellow glue, use it exclusively, and thoroughly learn its characteristics. Later, if you need to use another glue, you'll have something as a basis for comparison. (Gluing boards into panels—edge-jointing—is explained in Chapter Five.)

Two

MEASURING &
MARKING WOOD

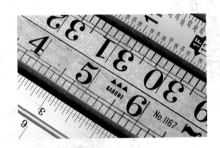

> *"Use accurate tools to mark and measure with.*
> *If possible, don't measure at all."*
>
> **—Frank Klaus*, during lunch with author**

Because any fine-furniture project begins with the marking of boards for dimensioning (and later for joint-making), it is obvious that precision in this first step is of primary importance if accurate work is to result. Marking out is one aspect of woodworking in which precision is essential.

Sometimes woodworkers throw terms around like "perfectly square" and "perfectly flat"; these terms don't really apply to wood. A flat board can absorb moisture overnight and be "less flat" in the morning than it was the night before, but still be quite usable. A cabinet carcass can be assembled a bit out of square (by 1/32 or 1/16 inch) and still be considered square. But marking and measuring *is* absolute—the board is either marked and measured correctly or it isn't. This isn't to say you should agonize over each mark. Marking and measuring should be done quickly and accurately.

The very best method doesn't involve measuring anything. You mark the dimensions on a *storypole*, which is a stick. Dimensions can be made directly from a piece of furniture, cabinet, etc. (**2–1**). Then the pole is used to transfer dimensions to the workpieces. Entire rooms—kitchens especially—can have all their important dimensions marked on storypoles, and then the craftsman can essentially "carry" the room back into the shop afterwards.

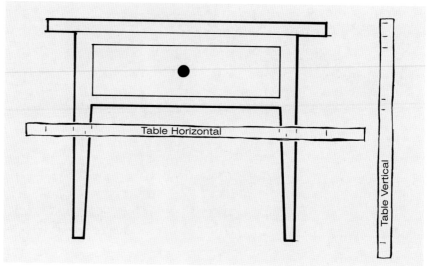

2–1. ◆ *A storypole allows you to mark directly (and more accurately) from a piece or from the space where the piece goes (i.e., a kitchen) without the accumulated errors that occur from writing down measurements.*

Table Horizontal

Table Vertical

*Frank Klaus, a New-Jersey cabinetmaker who also teaches woodworking seminars, produces woodworking videos, and has written extensively on the subject, learned the trade as an apprentice in Europe.

Storypoling eliminates errors that can either be made initially or accumulate when every dimension is measured and notated. And it's easier than measuring. The very best cabinetmaker I know puts it this way: "Mark, don't measure."

MEASURING AND MARKING TOOLS

As is so often the case in woodworking today, using well-made, quality tools is of paramount importance. Using the right tools for marking and measuring will immediately eliminate about 80 percent of the possible errors.

Of primary importance are the following tools, which are shown in **2–2**:

1. Combination Square. This is the most important measuring tool you can own *if you buy a good one.* Buy a combination square like the one shown. It is the best available. Dead accurate, rugged, and dependable, it does the work of about four or five other tools (**2–3** and **2–4**). A cheap one is worse than not having one at all, because bad information is worse than no information.

2. Folding Rule. I use a small, old-fashioned type made in England. It is much easier for bench work than a tape measure.

3. Tape Measure. Buy a ¾-inch-wide, 12- or 16-foot model (a 25- or 30-foot tape measure is too massive).

4. Mortise Gauge. This tool has a fence and two beams for marking mortises and tenons.

2–2. ◆ *The tools needed for measuring and marking wood. Clockwise from the top: a folding rule, marking knife, pencil, tape measure, combination square, and dividers.*

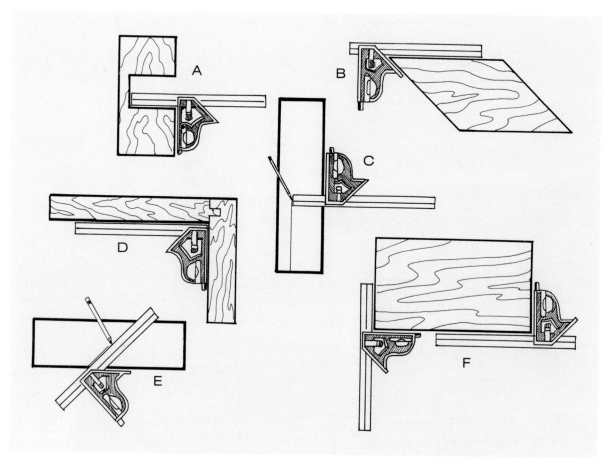

2–3. ◆ *A combination square can be set to mark work for all sorts of applications involving dimensioning or joint-making. It can be used: A, as a depth gauge; B, as a 45-degree-angle gauge; C, as a marking gauge; D, as a try square; E, to mark at 45 degrees; and F, to check a board for square.*

2–4. ◆ *Here, a combination square is used to mark a board for a rip cut with a handsaw.*

It can also be used as a straight marking gauge. Buy the Japanese type, which uses blades instead of pins (**2–5 to 2–7**). The blades make a clear, distinct line; Western pin gauges make scratchy marks (which are useless).

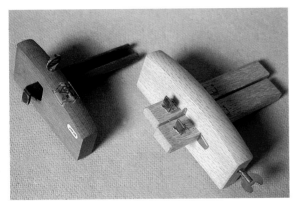

2–5. ◆ *Two types of Japanese marking (actually mortise) gauge. Either one will allow you to accurately mark one or two lines.*

5. Marking Knife. I use a red-handled X-acto hobby knife. The blades are replaceable and not too flimsy. A knife line is much more accurate than a pencil line.

6. Utility Knife. Use this tool when you need to make deeper, heavier lines than the marking knife can make. A retractable one is safer.

7. Pencil. A #2 is good. Keep it sharp. A carpenter's pencil is too wide and inaccurate for fine woodworking.

8. Dividers (optional). Useful for repetitive marking. Buy good ones that won't deflect or move out of adjustment.

Make sure you use the highest-quality tools possible. The best craftsmen I know use high-quality tools, and for good reason. Marking is the first step in the woodworking process. Small initial errors can be re-

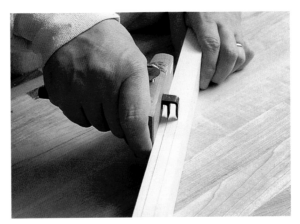

2–6 and 2–7. ◆ *Japanese marking gauges can mark single or double lines for a mortise.*

peated and accumulate into a gross inaccuracy later.

For example, I once compared two combination squares—a Starrett and a "bargain" brand made by a noted manufacturer (Contractor Grade, the manufacturer calls it). On the straight edge of a board, I made a line with the blade extended about 10 inches. Flipping the adjustable tongue to the other side of the blade, I made another line. The Starrett lines matched exactly. The tool is accurate. The bargain square made two lines that started in the same place, but extended up in a V shape.

The ends of the V were almost ⅛ inch from each other. That's a ¹⁄₁₆-inch error over 10 inches—a gross error. Use that square to mark out the four joints in a cabinet face or door frame and you could be off ¼ inch or more by the time you get to assembly! On a larger piece, the error would be much greater.

Real experts (not writers and talkers) use high-grade, quality tools because they are accurate and eliminate errors. The best there is is what you need.

SIMPLE TECHNIQUES

Marking and measuring procedures will be covered as they are needed in later chapters, but here are a few handy general techniques to know. They include techniques for dividing a board into equal parts, finding the center of boards, making a rip cut, making a V-shaped cut, and planing end grain.

Dividing a Board into Equal Parts

If the board you're dividing measures around 5¾ inches, for example, and you need to divide it into six parts, you don't have to calculate anything. Set the divider for about ¾ inch and "walk" it across the board. When, after six steps, it comes up short or long, judge by eye the total amount it is off by and either add or subtract one-sixth of this amount to the setting. By the third time through, you should have the exact distance (2–8).

Finding the Center of a Board

To find the center of a board's width, length, or thickness, first measure the total dimension you wish to halve. Let's say we want to halve the width, and you measure 4⁹⁄₁₆ inches for the total width. Set the combination square to about half of that—2⅜ inches. Now, make a mark from each side of the

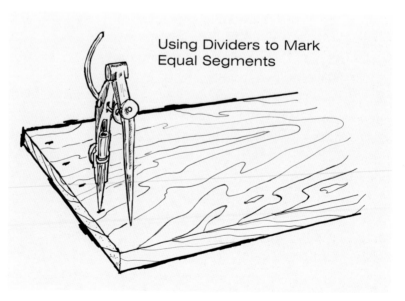

Using Dividers to Mark Equal Segments

2–8. ◆ *"Walking off" equal parts of a board with dividers. Judge the divisions of the total width by eye and adjust the parts until they are equally divided. This is much easier than calculating dimensions.*

board at that setting. *The marks will not match; there will be a space between them.* By eye, make another mark between the marks. That's the center of the board's width (**2–9**).

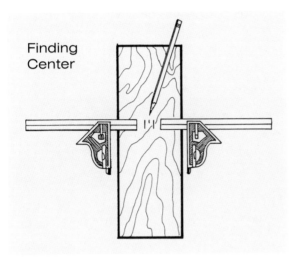

Finding Center

2–9. ◆ *A combination square can easily find the center of your board.*

Marking a Rip Cut (Parallel Line)

You can set any dimension you like on the combination square and draw a line the length of a board parallel to the straight edge. Hold a sharp pencil in contact with the end of the blade as you slide the assembly along the edge (**2–10**).

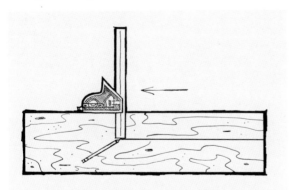

Marking a Board for a Rip Cut

Marking and Making a V-Cut

A V-cut (**2–11**) is useful for beginners first learning to crosscut boards by hand, but it is also necessary for joinery such as sliding dovetails, hand-cut rabbets, grooves, etc.

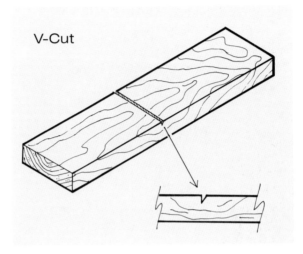

V-Cut

2–11. ◆ *A V-cut.*

With the board clamped down, first make a knife line across the grain with the marking knife (**2–12**). Hold the tongue against the board with your thumb, and your forefinger

2–12. ◆ *Marking a line with a marking knife.*

2–10. ◆ *A combination square can mark a line parallel to the edge of a board, as far as 10 inches.*

against the blade. The remaining three fingers rest on the board. The tongue must be tight against the edge, the blade flat against the face of the board, and the whole assembly still. Mark the line with the knife. With the light-duty marking knife, the line is thin; you don't use much pressure.

Next, take the utility knife and deepen the line (2–13). Make two or three passes, using more pressure as you go deeper. Be relaxed, and watch your fingers. If you tense up, the knife can slip. Using a chisel, cut a V-shaped groove to one side of the line (2–14). The saw blade will rest in this groove as you make the crosscut (2–15 and 2–16).

2–13. ◆ Deepen the line with a utility knife.

2–14. ◆ Using a chisel to make the V-cut.

2–15. ◆ The finished V-cut.

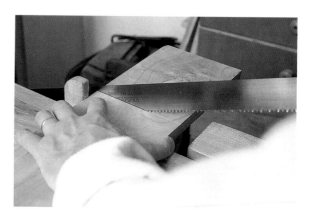

2–16. ◆ The saw blade rests in the V-cut and it's easy to saw cleanly and accurately.

Marking Techniques for Planing End Grain

The method described here is used often in cabinetwork. The marking is just as responsible for a good result as the planing is. With a marking knife, make a mark around the board. Deepen it with a utility knife. Now the board can be sawn about 1/16 to 1/8 inch beyond the cut (on the waste side, of course). Clamp the board upright in the vise and plane to the lines with a sharp, low-angle block plane (2–17).

Plane from the middle in so you don't tear out the end fibers. First plane the left side. You'll know when to stop when you see the marking line (2–18). Now do the same thing with the right side. You now have a hump of end grain in the middle with both sides planed down to the marking line. Plane the middle flat and you're finished (2–19).

SUMMARY

Accurate marking saves much time and trouble. Good marking lines, made with a knife, are part of the joint-cutting process. When planing end grain, the lines will show you when to stop. With joint-making, the success of the joint is determined when it's marked. Do it correctly and the joints will fit.

One teacher of mine said, "Cutting this joint isn't that tough. If you can mark it well, you can cut it."

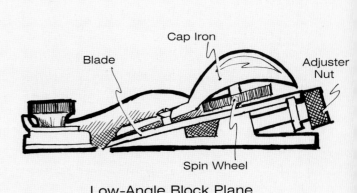

Low-Angle Block Plane Cutaway View

2–17. ◆ *A low-angle block plane. Not a measuring tool, it's used to plane end grain. However, the measuring is as much a part of the operation as the planing. The low blade angle is optimum for this work.*

2–18. ◆ *"Blocking in" with the block plane until the lines show you where to stop.*

2–19. ◆ *End grain planed properly to the line.*

SAWING TO A LINE

"Sawing by hand? A bow saw is best. Ja."

Tage Frid*

T his is perhaps the most essential skill in the craft of woodworking. Not being able to saw accurately to a cut line with a handsaw reflects an embarrassing lack of competence. It means that for every board cut to length or ripped to width, for every panel sawn to length, and for every joint you ever cut—tenon, dovetail, or even a *haunch*—you have to rely on a machine. That is the equivalent of a pianist's being unable to play without automatic accompaniment from an electronic keyboard.

It's simply ridiculous to use a machine to cut ¼ inch of material, but lots of people do it. A woodworking "expert" once suggested to me that a stack dado head be used to cut haunches on four tenons! Incredible. In the time it would have taken just to unbolt the blade from the table saw to switch to the dado head, the haunches on all four tenons could have been cut with a handsaw.

When another woodworker or a student tells me they can't get a handsaw to cut well or that it's cutting too slowly, I know that either they are using the wrong saw or the saw is sharpened and set incorrectly. Usually it's both. This chapter will address the types of saw to use and methods for determining and adjusting the degree of set in the blade. Sharpening a dull blade is covered in Chapter Four.

THE BOW SAW

The all-around cabinetmaker's saw in continental Europe is the bow saw (**3–1**). All of the craftspeople from continental Europe I have met or spoken to were trained with one. They use it for everything—dimensioning, ripping, and crosscutting boards, jointmaking, cutting curves, etc. Why it remains an obscure item in the United States is a profound mystery to me. With two bow saws, you could do all the sawing necessary to make an entire piece of furniture.

The bow saw is the best saw there is, for several reasons. First of all, it cuts very fast (if a saw cuts slowly, it's useless). Also, the blade is held in tension in a frame, so it won't whip or kink as you cut, like the standard carpenter's handsaw does**. Because it's held in tension, the blade is very thin. This helps it cut not only quickly, but accurately (**3–2** and **3–3**). And a bow saw's blade design is also very forgiving—it's easy even for beginners to sharpen.

Before I continue, there are some general misconceptions often mentioned with regard to bow saws in woodworking literature that should be addressed. The most common is

*Tage Frid is a former Professor of Woodworking at Rochester Institute of Technology and at Rhode Island School of Design.

**Japanese crosscut and rip saws, used on the *pull* rather than push stroke, have thin blades which—being pulled—also do not whip or kink. They work well. The teeth configurations, however, are delicate and difficult to set and sharpen.

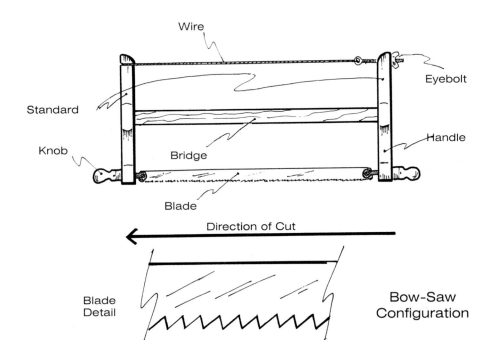

Wire

Eyebolt

Standard

Handle

Knob

Bridge

Blade

Direction of Cut

Blade
Detail

Bow-Saw
Configuration

3–1. ◆ A cabi-
netmaker's bow
saw (German
type). At set-up,
align the handle
end with the eye-
bolt; this way,
you'll always
know which end
to grasp.

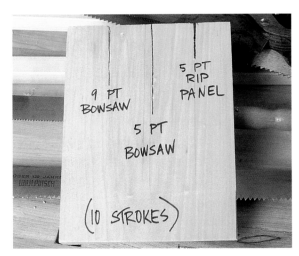

3–2. ◆ Comparing a bow saw's speed of cut when ripping (cutting with the grain) to a panel saw's (standard
carpenter's handsaw). In ten strokes, a 5-point bow
saw cut more than twice as far as a panel saw with the
same number of teeth per inch. A 9-point joint-making
bow saw with almost twice the points (teeth) per inch
cuts about twice as far.

3–3. ◆ Comparing a bow saw's speed of cut when
crosscutting (cutting against the grain) to panel saws'.
The panel saws, with 5 and 9 points per inch, do a little better crosscutting than making rip cuts, but the
bow-saw results are still clearly superior.

that a bow saw comes only with a narrow blade and is used only to cut curves (scroll-cutting). Not true. Bow-saw blades come in 1½-inch widths, with large and small teeth, as well as in narrow scroll-saw widths, and are used for rip-cutting and crosscutting, as well as scroll-cutting. Also untrue is the idea that the harp-like English bow saw is the only type available. In my experience, these saws are pretty looking but just about impossible to hold and just as difficult to do any work with.

The best bow saws are made in Germany. As shown in **3–1**, they use a wire and eyebolt to tension the blade rather than string and a wooden pin. This is an advantage—you don't need to loosen the string when you're done using it. The other type comes from Denmark and is smaller; it is used for cutting joints and other small work. The Danish model uses string and a wooden pin for tension.

I would buy a large German bow saw with a 28-inch, 5-point-per-inch* blade and one with a 20-inch, 9-point-per-inch blade (the 20-inch German models may be difficult to find). I would also buy a Danish model with the 9-point blade (**3–4**). I keep an extra blade on hand for each saw.

Another point: Buy your bow saws, don't make them—especially from old band-saw blades. A band-saw blade is too narrow for a cabinetmaker's bow saw, and even if it weren't, the configuration of the teeth is all wrong for a handsaw. The Europeans have been making quality bow saws and blades for

centuries, and they are inexpensive. Utilize their expertise. You are (hopefully!) striving to be a skilled woodworking craftsman, not an amateur manufacturer.

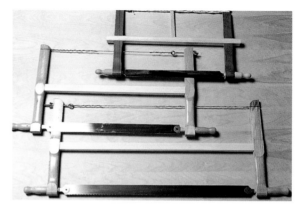

3–4. ◆ *The bow saws I use in my shop. With these saws, woodworkers can do remarkable things. Bottom: German 28-inch, 5-point-per-inch bow saw. Middle: German 20-inch, 9-point-per-inch bow saw. Top: Danish 16-inch, 9-point-per-inch bow saw. (American inch indications are approximate.)*

RIP AND CROSSCUT TEETH

You will read that there are crosscut saws (and blades) designed to cut across the grain and rip saws (and blades) designed to cut with the grain. With regard to the bow saw, these distinctions can be ignored. All sharpening configurations will be for rip cutting.

Crosscut-blade profiles were originally used to prevent carpenters from tearing out the fibers in wet framing lumber. Since we use dry hardwoods for cabinetmaking, the rip profile works better (faster) for both ripping and crosscutting. All a crosscut-blade profile will do is slow down the cutting.

---

*Points per inch refers to the amount of teeth there are per inch. For example, a 9-point blade has 9 teeth per inch.

SET

Set is the amount of offset the teeth have from each other. If you look directly at the teeth in any saw blade, you can see that they go in alternate directions—one goes to the left, the next goes to the right, etc. That is the set. The amount that they go left and right is the *degree* of set.

Most saws come with too much set. Illus. 3–5 shows a 5-point blade with too much set.

3–6. ◆ *One tap per tooth from the small peen on a ball-peen hammer will remove excess set in a saw blade.*

3–5. ◆ *This blade's teeth show far too much "set" for cutting dry hardwoods.*

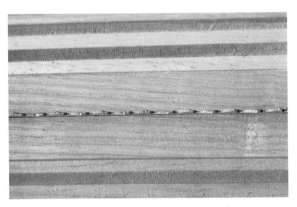

3–7. ◆ *These 5-point bow-saw teeth have the proper amount of set. They look like they have no set at all.*

The more set a blade has, the slower it cuts (excess set is good, however, for cutting green, or "wet," wood). To remove excess set from a saw blade, lay the blade flat on a metalworker's anvil and *lightly* tap down the teeth that are sticking up. First do one side, and then the other. Most inexpensive metalworking vises have a little flat anvil surface behind the jaws that works well for this (3–6).

The proper amount of set is almost invisible. As you look at a properly set bow-saw blade, the teeth should barely be discernibly offset from one another (3–7). A small turned-handle saw, sometimes called a dovetail or "gents" saw (3–8), really needs no set since its maximum depth of cut is only about

Turned-Handle Dovetail or "Gents" Saw

3–8. ◆ *A turned-handle "gents" saw. Also called a dovetail saw, this saw is useful for trimming and cutting very small pieces of wood. Sharpen with triangular needle files. The teeth should have almost no set.*

¾ inch. Once you tap the set out, you can leave it as is.

Some German bow saws come with 5-point blades that have the right amount of set. These are manufactured by W. Putsch. Putsch blades don't need resetting. One American tool dealer sells bow saws from Germany. All the blades have too much set and must be tapped down and reset. The Danish bow-saw blades also must be reset.

One last point about bow saws: Because the blades are enclosed in a frame, they must be long enough so that you have enough "throw" as you cut. ("Throw" is the length of the cutting stroke.) A bow saw for ripping and crosscutting stock to dimension (5-point) must be at least 27 inches long; 30 inches is better. My 20-inch bow saw has a 9-point blade and is used for cutting joints—tenons, bridle joints, thick dovetails, etc. (This is shown in Chapter Six.) The 16-inch, 9-point Danish bow saw performs the same function.

Don't try using a narrow scroll-saw blade for straight cuts (it wanders in the work and won't cut straight), and don't use a short-bladed bow saw for sizeable work.

TOOLS FOR SETTING SAW TEETH

These tools are called saw sets; the easiest ones to use resemble a squatty pair of pliers (3–9). I use one made by Stanley for larger-toothed saws, and a Japanese model made by Somax (a #250) for smaller teeth. In use, the saw tooth is clamped against a round anvil and a plunger pushes the tooth forward onto the anvil, creating the set (3–10). The anvil

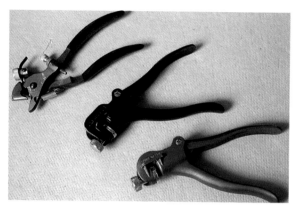

3–9. ◆ *Saw sets. The middle and bottom saw sets are easy to use. The top one is a German model that's a bit more difficult to use.*

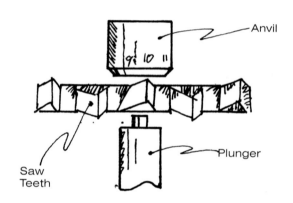

3–10. ◆ *The workings of a saw set. With the blade clamped in the plier jaws, the plunger pushes a saw tooth against a beveled anvil to bend each tooth the same amount.*

has a graduated bevel going around it. The lower numbers on the anvil are for more set; higher numbers are for less set. There is no correlation between the numbers on the anvil and the number of teeth per inch.

For 5-point bow-saw blades set on the Stanley tool, I position the anvil at the #12 setting (3–11). For 9-point blades set on the Somax tool, I use a position between the 9 and the 10 (**3–12**). With the saw clamped lightly in the bench, I tilt the blade and teeth toward me and set them (**3–13**).

As a general rule, you won't need to reset the teeth until they've been sharpened at least three or four times. If you have a Putsch bow saw, just leave it as it is when you get it. With any other bow saw or a turned-handle (gents) saw, tap out the set and leave the saw as is.

3–11. ◆ *The saw set at the proper setting for 5-point bow-saw teeth.*

3–12. ◆ *The saw set (for smaller teeth) at the proper setting for 9-point bow-saw teeth.*

3–13. ◆ *Setting saw teeth. Here I'm using the Stanley saw set on my 5-point bow saw. The saw set pushes the teeth away from you, so do one side, turn the saw around, and then do the other.*

SAWING TO A CUT LINE

To *crosscut* with a bow saw, first make a V-cut across the board, as described in Chapter Three. Then pick up the saw and check that the blade is straight and not twisted. Align the blade straight with the frame.

Holding the saw is important. There is a general belief that a tight grip on the saw creates power in the cut, but it does not. Hold the saw lightly. Pretend you're holding a baby bird (golfers will appreciate this): too little pressure and the bird will fly away; too much and you crush the bird.

Hold the saw on the line with your thumb. Pull the saw back the length of the blade to start the cut. Now push forward, cutting the wood along the line (3–14). As you near the end of the cut, hold the board down with your left elbow and reach through the saw to hold the piece to the right so it won't fall off and splinter as you finish the cut.

For a *rip* cut, mark a pencil line with the combination square (easier to see with the grain) a set distance from a straight edge on a board. Clamp the board in the bench vertically. Tilt the blade at a slight angle so it will clear the board as you cut (3–15). Align the blade with your thumb, pull the saw back, and cut as before.

When either ripping or crosscutting, use

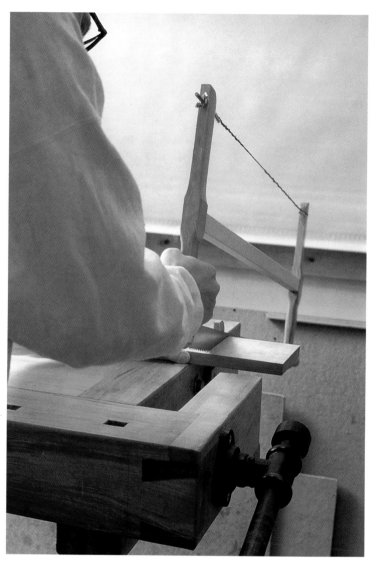

3–14. ◆ *Crosscutting with a bow saw. If you grip the bow saw loosely and pay attention on the cutting line, the bow saw will seem to almost cut by itself.*

the *entire* blade. Take long strokes. Each stroke should use almost all the teeth in the blade.

When you first start cutting with a bow saw, it may seem a bit ponderous and top-heavy. There isn't any quick tip or advice I can suggest that can make it cut faster or more easily. It's a matter of getting used to the saw. A good woodworker with a bow saw can press an average table-saw user pretty hard.

You should master the use of a bow saw. Here's how. Take a stack of boards (about two feet long and five inches wide) and make 50 crosscuts and 50 ripcuts in a row. Not four cuts—50. Spend two or three hours. It beats being a machine operator for the rest of your life. When you're done, you'll be able to do something only about two percent of woodworkers in the United States can do.

3–15. ◆ *Rip-sawing with a bow saw. A bow-saw blade can be turned at an angle to the frame to clear the board for work like this. These saws cut so well you can do entire projects with them.*

SHARPENING TOOLS

"A sharp blade is more important than the horsepower."

Arthur Chapin*

One of my earliest memories in woodworking is of learning how to sharpen properly. My teacher not only sharpened plane and chisel blades, but saw blades, knives, fishhooks, carving tools—anything. He would talk for hours about things like carbon steel, the temper of the steel, quenching the blade, and, most of all, the horrors of a dull cutting edge. Today, if he walks into my shop and picks up a cutting tool that isn't razor-sharp, I'll get the whole lesson all over again—including the part about how the ancient Romans would test their newly sharpened swords by running them through a slave's body! (I don't recommend that.)

Using properly sharpened tools is important. Eighty to ninety percent of problems when using planes, for example, come from a dull blade. Chisel use is difficult and dangerous unless the tool is sharp, and nothing is worse than trying to cut with a dull handsaw. In most of the woodworking literature, these skills are often shown to be unnecessarily complicated. Learning to sharpen tools correctly is straightforward.

4–1. ◆ *Left to right: slim file for 5-point blades; double extra-slim (XX) file for 9-point blades; 9-point bow-saw blade; and 5-point bow-saw blade.*

SHARPENING HANDSAWS

Once the set on a handsaw blade is correct (see previous chapter), it is important to keep the teeth sharp. To sharpen them, you use a triangular file that fits the tooth size (**4–1**), filing at 90 degrees to the blade. It isn't necessary to turn the blade around and file from both sides, nor is a crosscut-tooth profile ever necessary. Why have you never heard this before? I don't know. These techniques have worked beautifully in my shop for many years, and they'll work well for you, too.

*Arthur Chapin is a woodworker and craftsman living in Fairport, New York.

How do you know when a saw blade is dull? Look at it. The tips of a dull saw blade will reflect light, so you will see tiny points of light glinting off the teeth (**4–2**). A sharp tooth has no forward edge, so no light glints off it. It ends in a sharp point. From now on, wherever you are, you can pick up a steel saw blade (or any steel cutting edge, for that matter), look at the teeth, and tell easily if it's sharp or dull.

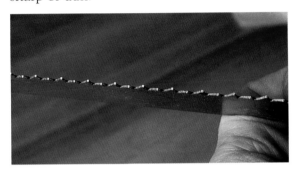

Since I use handsaws every day, I check them about once every two weeks. At the first sign of light on the points of the teeth, I sharpen them.

SAW VISE

You'll need a sharpening vise to keep the blade clamped tightly while you file it. Some of the photographs illustrate one that Tage Frid showed me how to make some years ago. I still use it, but I've since designed a vise (**4–3**) that has some advantages. The most important one

4–2. ◆ *To determine if the blade is sharp, look at it. This saw blade is dull—there are visible edges on the ends of the teeth that reflect light.*

4–3. ◆ *This sharpening vise—which can be easily made—makes filing saw teeth easy. The rubber jaws are highly effective in holding the steel saw blade firmly with a moderate amount of clamp pressure.*

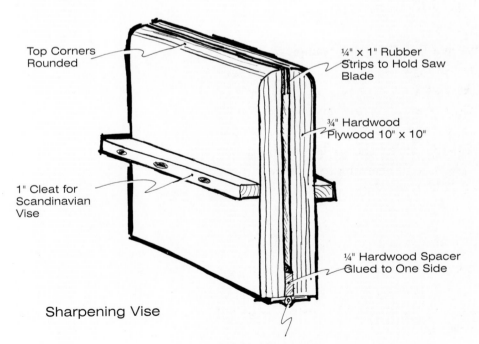

Top Corners Rounded

¼" x 1" Rubber Strips to Hold Saw Blade

¾" Hardwood Plywood 10" x 10"

1" Cleat for Scandinavian Vise

¼" Hardwood Spacer Glued to One Side

Sharpening Vise

Butt or Piano Hinge

is that the jaws that hold the saw blade are made of rubber. These are much more efficient than the wooden jaws on the Frid vise. When the rubber jaws grip the blade, they hold it much tighter with less pressure. The spacer, glued to one of the lower portions, insures that the rubber jaws maintain an even, tight grip on the blade, and that the blade will not slip.

Another advantage is that the top edges are simply rounded with a rasp and then sanded, or you can just sand them. These rounded edges allow you to get your hand close while working, and are comfortable when your hand brushes them. This vise will hold the blade nice and tight, and allow you to file saw blades easily.

If you use an English-style bench vise, you don't need the cleats on the vise sides. The cleats rest on the upper part of Scandinavian-type bench jaws and prevent the vise from falling onto the floor.

To make one, start with two 10 × 10-inch pieces of hardwood plywood (birch, oak, etc.) (4–4). A cabinet shop will have them as scrap. I use ¾-inch lumber-core lauan plywood, and that works well also. Just don't use sheathing or decking (construction) plywood.

You'll also need two small butt hinges (I use a scrap of piano hinge), a hot-melt glue gun, and two 1 × 10-inch scraps of ⅛-inch-thick rubber gasket material. If you have trouble getting the gasket material, you can use an old inner tube from a large tire or get thinner pieces from a bicycle shop and glue them together to make them thicker. The spacer block should equal the thickness of the rubber jaws when they're glued on the plywood pieces; in this case, it's ¼ inch thick. In Illus. 4–4, the spacer is already glued onto one of the plywood pieces.

With everything ready, spread hot-melt glue on the inside top of one of the pieces of

4–4. ◆ *Materials necessary for making a sharpening vise: plywood pieces, rubber strips, hinges (a scrap of piano hinge is shown here), hot-melt glue gun, and screwdriver. Note that the spacer piece is already glued to one of the pieces of plywood.*

plywood (4–5). Spread it so there will be glue along the entire width of the rubber piece. Press the rubber piece down evenly on the still-hot glue (4–6). Be sure there is good contact all along the length and width of the piece. Do this with both rubber pieces. Next, screw the hinges onto the bottom of the two pieces to make a vise (4–7). You'll find this vise ideal for the long blades on bow saws, as well as for all types of handsaws (4–8).

4–5. ◆ *Spreading hot-melt glue to adhere the rubber jaws to the plywood. Cleaning the rubber pieces is a good idea. Work quickly!*

4–6. ◆ *Pressing the rubber jaw into position on the inside top of the plywood piece.*

4–7. ◆ *Attaching the hinge with screws. Two small cabinet butt hinges will also work in place of the piano hinge shown here.*

4–8. ◆ *The vise about to be put to use. The rubber jaws lock the saw blade tightly in place. Note the lower cleat, which holds the vise up against the Scandinavian workbench. If you're using an English-style vise, you don't need it.*

FILING A BOW SAW

Another advantage of the bow saw is that the teeth are relatively large, so the files used to sharpen them are easy to find. For a 5-point blade, a "slim" size works well (refer to **4–1**); for a 9-point blade, use a "double extra-slim" file. You can usually find them in hardware stores or home centers. (For dovetail and "gents" saws, you'll need *needle files* [**4–9**].) I use a piece of dowel as a handle (**4–10**), rounding over the bottom edge a little with a rasp. You can also use a piece of tree branch.

To file the saw blade, clamp it in the vise (you can leave it in the bow-saw frame). Take a piece of chalk and chalk the file on two edges (**4–11**). The chalk keeps the file working better longer. Place the chalked edges of the file in the triangular recess and file at 90 degrees to the saw blade (**4–12**).

4–9. ◆ *Needle file (chalked) shown above the wood rule. These tiny files are used to sharpen the very small gents-saw teeth. An easy, gentle touch is called for when filing these saw teeth.*

4–10. ◆ *Files for sharpening handsaws. I use pieces of dowel for handles (old, discarded foam-brush handles work well). Round over the ends for comfort. Shown on top is a handle I made from a tree branch.*

4–11. ◆ *Chalking the file on two edges.*

4–12. ◆ *With the blade at a comfortable height, one or two strokes per tooth will get it nice and sharp. The file is perpendicular to the saw blade's horizontal and vertical axes.*

You are filing the front of one tooth and the back of another at the same time. Start at the front end and work back toward the handle. There is no need to flip the saw around as advised in some books—just file from the front to the back (handle), as shown in **4–13**. We are filing a rip-tooth configuration here; hence the straight file angle. There is no need to ever use a crosscut configuration on a handsaw. It is unnecessary.

Filing a Bow-saw Blade

4–13. ◆ *Sharpening a bow saw. Use enough pressure to keep the file "biting" into the steel. The file is at 90 degrees to the blade, top and side. Most first-timers use too much pressure.*

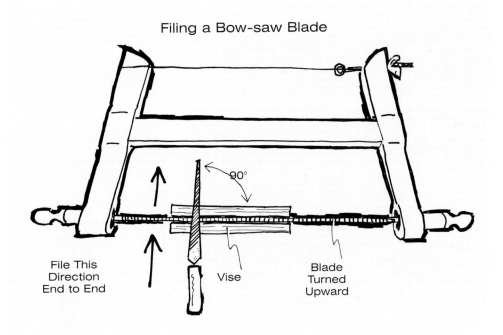

90°

File This
Direction
End to End

Vise

Blade
Turned
Upward

Use only enough downward (not side-to-side) pressure to allow the file to bite into the steel. Most first-timers use too much pressure. Hold the file by the handle and the tip and be relaxed as you work. One stroke per tooth is enough if only a bit of light glints off the teeth. Use the same edges of the file for the entire blade. If the file "skates" and doesn't bite, the file is old, the blade isn't clamped tight enough, or you aren't using sufficient pressure. Don't attempt to use a lot of force with a worn file. Get a new one.

Consistency is important (**4–14**). If you aren't consistent with your strokes and pressure, the teeth will be at uneven heights and only the high teeth will do any cutting. A bow saw will still work well, even if you aren't completely consistent at first, but a backsaw or a panel saw will stall and jam in the wood and be very difficult to use if the teeth aren't even. Still, don't

freeze up. Relax and you'll be able to file accurately.

When you've finished sharpening the bow-saw teeth, don't stone their edges—that's more gross misinformation someone dreamed up. Just leave them as is. If there is a burr, three or four strokes through your first board will remove it.

SHARPENING CHISELS AND PLANE IRONS

Some chisel- and plane-iron sharpening methods will leave a "better" (i.e., longer-lasting) edge than others, and some methods take longer to do than others, but the objective is always the same—a razor-sharp edge. To tell if the edge on your chisel or plane is sharp enough, with a *very light motion* try to shave the hair from your forearm. If you can, it is. If not, it will have to be sharpened.

I've tried almost all types of sharpening technique and equipment over the years, and settled on Japanese water stones some time ago. In not too much time, they leave a quality, long-lasting, razor-sharp edge. There are different ways to use them, however, and some can be confusing. Therefore, I will describe a very quick and easy method using diamond stones and a leather strop (**4–15**). Though not providing quite as long-lasting an edge as the water stones, the diamond-and-strop technique will obtain a razor-sharp edge faster and with less effort. This is not to say it is an inferior technique; it is a fine sharpening method you can use for your entire career if you like.

4–14. ◆ *These teeth have been properly filed (sharpened). They are all the same height, so all of them do some of the cutting.*

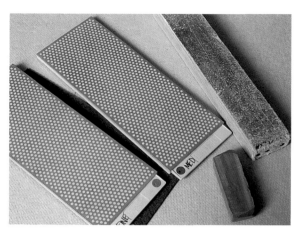

4–15. ◆ *Diamond sharpening "stones," a leather strop, and buffing (or stropping) compound. I use double-side diamond stones, which have one coarse-grit side and one extra-fine-grit side. You can use just a medium grit if you like.*

4–16. ◆ *The grinder in my shop. The block of wood on the left wheel is for grinding straight edges before grinding a bevel with the tool rest on the right wheel. A good tool rest is very important.*

Grinding the Bevel

A new chisel or plane iron doesn't need grinding. You can proceed right to honing (using diamond stones and a strop, as discussed on pages 70 to 73). Otherwise, the blade will need an even 25-degree bevel on one edge.

My grinder (**4–16**) cost twenty dollars new many years ago. For a long time, I used it with the gray wheels that came with it. Later I put on one cool-running white, aluminum-oxide wheel.

The most important items related to power grinding are a good tool rest and a wheel dresser. The tool rest keeps the tool at the desired bevel angle; the wheel dresser cleans the wheel of metal particles and keeps the face of it flat*. The tool rest on my grinder cost twice what the grinder cost, and is absolutely essential. Again, don't shortcut this step.

A bench grinder like the one shown is a simple and easy-to-use piece of equipment, but be sure to take proper safety precautions. The tool rest insures that the blade is braced and safe while the wheel grinds it. Never grind a blade without a tool rest. Keep your fingers from contacting the wheel; it can grind through skin quickly. Have plenty of light whenever you grind a blade, and, most important, wear eye protection. Most grinders come with clear guards, but I use safety glasses anyway. Flying particles of metal are very dangerous to the eyes. Make sure you protect them.

---

*As the wheel clogs with steel particles, it will cut slower and heat the steel faster. This is when you "dress" it. My wheels require "dressing" once for about every five or six tools sharpened.

The first step in grinding a blade is to draw a straight line across the back of the blade, as close to the top as you can get it (**4–17**). Use a micro-point, permanent marker. With the tool rest at 90 degrees to the wheel, gently grind to the line. Look at the cutting edge—about ⅟₁₆ inch of light will be glinting off it (**4–18**). Reset the tool rest at about 25 degrees to the wheel and have a can of water nearby to quench the blade. You can use the chisel's existing bevel to reset the tool rest (**4–19**).

Hold the chisel or plane iron as shown in **4–20**, with one finger near the top so you can feel the heat. Only the bevel is ground, not the back. What you want is an absolutely even, flawless, 25-degree bevel. Place the blade on the tool rest and slowly ease it into the wheel, using your other hand to move it from side to side. Use a light touch, and a relaxed motion. When you feel a slight bit of heat, dip the blade in the water can. Repeat until the light glinting off the cutting edge is

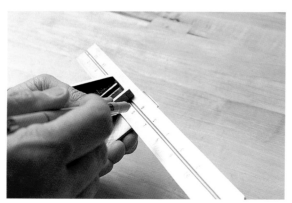

4–17. ◆ *Drawing a straight line on the back of a chisel blade. You will grind to this line.*

4–18. ◆ *The light clearly glinting off the edge of the chisel blade after grinding to the line reveals that it's very dull. The next step is to grind the bevel until this line is about the width of a human hair—without burning the steel.*

4–19. ◆ *Setting the tool rest using the existing bevel on the chisel. The bevel angle doesn't have to be precise. It should be about 25 degrees; a few degrees either way is fine.*

4–20. ◆ *Grinding the bevel. The large, flat, bearing surface of the tool rest makes it easy to get an even bevel. When my fingers feel warm, I quench the blade in water. Note the sparks.*

the width of a sharp pencil line. Don't grind the blade further than this—it's too easy to overheat it. Since the wheel is round, the bevel you've just ground is curved; it's a *hollow-ground* bevel (**4–21**).

Time for a digression. When I taught sharpening classes in St. Louis, students always seemed to bring rusty, ancient, poor-quality blades to class. I made them buy new ones. You can't do good work with old, decrepit tools, and you hopefully care enough about your woodworking skills that you wouldn't try to.

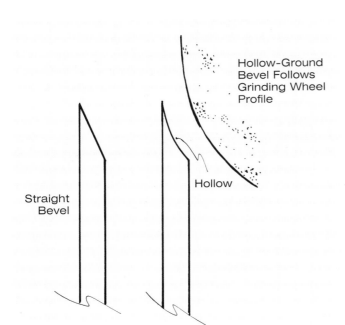

Hollow-Ground Bevel Follows Grinding Wheel Profile

Straight Bevel

Hollow

4–21. ◆ *The grinding wheel grinds a hollow in the bevel; hence the term hollow ground.*

Honing

Honing is where we take the blade from rough-ground to razor-sharp. Grinding leaves a burr on the back of the bevel (**4–22**). We'll remove it, create a "microbevel" on the freshly ground bevel, and "strop" it.

Diamond stones are the easiest way to hone a cutting edge. You can get by with just a medium-grit stone, but it helps to also have a fine-grit one. Best is to have all four:

coarse, medium, fine, and extra fine. A strop is a piece of thick leather, tacked "flesh side" out to a hardwood block, as shown in **4–15**. You'll need some stropping compound designed for carbon steel. That's it.

I put a pad under my knees and kneel on the floor with the diamond stone in front of me, propped up on a holder so it won't move. A water bottle and a towel are nearby. The stones I use come with the holder shown, but you can make a holder out of wood, or use a rubber pad, etc. Lay the chisel back flat on the stone and rub it back and forth to remove the burr (**4–23**). Wash the steel particles (swarf) off the stone with water (**4–24**).

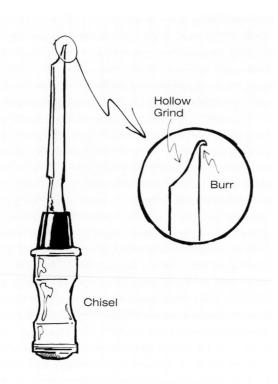

4–22. ◆ *The burr is a rough, turned-over edge on the back of a blade that's been created through power grinding. It's easier to feel it than to see it.*

4–23. ◆ *Honing the back of a chisel. I do this kneeling on the floor, my knees resting on a mat.*

4–24. ◆ *Washing the swarf off a diamond stone after use. This is about the only maintenance these things require. Dry the stone when you're done or the "ground" surface will rust.*

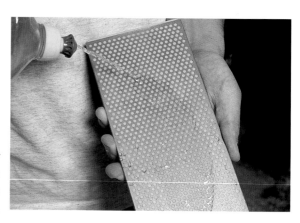

Turn the chisel over and rest the top and bottom edges of the bevel on the stone (4–25). Now lift the chisel a tiny bit so that only the front edge bears on the stone. Keeping this angle constant, rub the blade up and down the stone to create a microbevel* (4–26). You're finished when you can no longer see the tiny pencil line of light glinting off the edge. Wash the stone again and dry it (otherwise, it will rust).

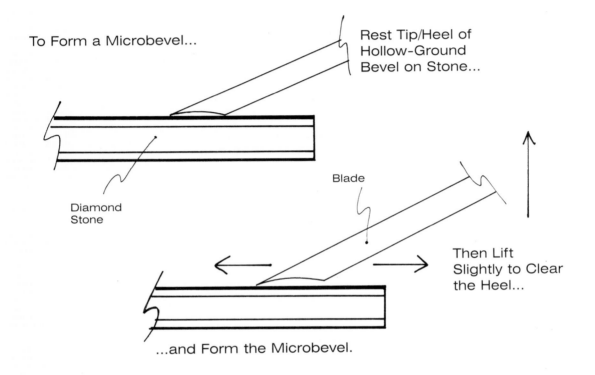

To Form a Microbevel...

Rest Tip/Heel of Hollow-Ground Bevel on Stone...

Diamond Stone

Blade

Then Lift Slightly to Clear the Heel...

...and Form the Microbevel.

4–25. ◆ *A microbevel on the edge of the hollow-ground bevel can be made quickly and works well.*

4–26. ◆ *Honing the microbevel. The grip is firm, but relaxed. When the hairline of light no longer glints off the edge, this step is done.*

*If you have four stones, stone the back with all four stones, but use only the fine and extra-fine stones to create the microbevel.

The stropping motion is always toward you—*away* from, not *into* the leather (**4–27**). This way, you won't slice into it. With the strop in front of you, rub some of the compound on it. Lay the chisel back on the strop and pull it toward you about five or six times (**4–28**). The strop will darken as you do this. Look at the chisel back. It should show some bright polish near the edge. Apply a little more compound and strop the microbevel, pulling toward you as before and keeping the angle constant (**4–29**). Three or four swipes should produce a bright, mirror-like microbevel.

Test the edge. *Very lightly*, try to shave a bit of hair from your forearm (**4–30**). Don't cut yourself; a light whisking is all you need. When the hair shaves off, congratulate yourself: you have achieved a razor-sharp edge. You can sharpen tools.

Stropping a Blade

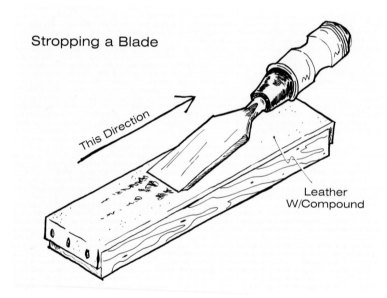

This Direction

Leather W/Compound

4–27. ◆ *"Stropping" the bevel edge. The motion is toward you, keeping the angle constant. You are polishing the very edge of the bevel to achieve a razor-sharp edge.*

4–28. ◆ *Stropping the back of the chisel blade. The motion is inward, toward me. The strop is shown here clamped in the workbench, for clarity.*

4–29. ◆ *Stropping the microbevel. You can see in this photograph the very slight lifting of the edge so the strop will contact the microbevel.*

4–30. ◆ *When the blade can shave hair from the forearm (use a light motion to do this), the tool is razor-sharp. This is how sharp all your edge tools should be.*

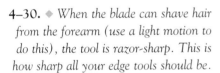

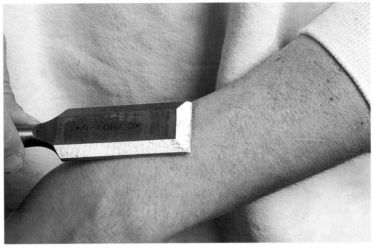

"Any worker must first reach an advanced level of competence before he can even begin to approach the richer possibilities of whatever medium he is involved with."

Fred Picker*, 1979

At about the five- or six-week point in the hand-tool class I teach, I will usually say something like this to the students: "I'd like you to make a board square, surfaced, and flat. I want the thickness to be 7⁄16 inch, the width to be 5⅛ inches, and the length to be 22¹⁄16 inches. There is a woodpile over there; use any wood you like. Just make sure it's not white pine or spruce (framing lumber). You have 40 minutes. Begin, please."

I had a visitor in class, also a woodworker. He expected screams of horror and protest, but instead students just got their hand planes ready and quietly made their way to the woodpile. "Can they do that?" he asked. He didn't quite believe it. "Yes, of course," I answered.

Those students were able to square, surface, and flatten wood with hand planes because they had the proper tools (**5–1**) and knew how to use them. If you pay attention to the information in this chapter, you too will be able to use hand planes as successfully as my students.

THE VALUE OF USING HIGH-QUALITY PLANES

Shaving wood from boards by hand is something of a precision operation. If the plane isn't in good condition, it won't work well.

5–1. ◆ *Removing scrub-plane marks with a jack plane. Most difficulties with hand-plane use stem from poorly manufactured tools and/or using the wrong plane for a given job.*

The soles on most new standard-grade planes—even smooth and block planes—aren't close to flat. This means you can't make a proper (thin) shaving. Also, the blades get dull quickly and the cap iron that fits over the blade isn't ground flat to the blade. Shavings jam in there and stall the tool on the work. Can you fix it? Yes. But you'll have to take it to a machine shop to flatten the sole, file and grind the cap iron, and heaven knows what else. Modern standard-grade planes could also be called "poor-quality" planes.

Save yourself the difficulty. Buy the best planes you can—planes made for serious work. Buy good planes at the outset, so you

---

*Fred Picker is a photographer and writer living in Putney, Vermont.

can spend your time on woodworking and furnituremaking—not tinkering with junky tools. You can't do serious work with these types of tool.

Lie-Nielsen Toolworks in the United States and E.C. Emmerich in Germany make high-quality planes. Lie-Nielsen makes metal planes, and E.C. Emmerich wooden ones. The planes work beautifully, right out of the box.

TUNING AND ADJUSTING STANDARD-GRADE HAND PLANES

For standard-grade hand planes such as the jack plane shown in this section (**5–2** and **5–3**), some tuning and adjustment is necessary before the plane will even work at all. First of all, the blade must be sharp. That's simple

5–2. ◆ *A standard-grade jack plane. These tools are inexpensive, but their quality can limit performance. Cap-iron stoning and blade sharpening are the minimum things to do to get them to work at all.*

5–3. ◆ *Standard-quality planes suffer from blades that are too thin, imprecise "seating" of the frog on the body and the blade assembly, and soles that aren't flat.*

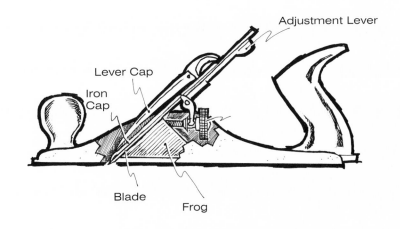

Adjustment Lever

Lever Cap

Iron Cap

Blade

Frog

"Standard" Jack Plane
Simplified View

enough to do. Refer to the previous chapter for instruction on how to achieve this.

Second, the cap iron—the piece that screws to the plane blade to hold it rigid— must fit tightly to the blade (5–4). If the cap iron isn't snug where it meets the blade, shavings will jam in there and the plane will stall. To get a tight fit, use a coarse diamond stone (as described in the previous chapter) to achieve a slight relief behind the surface that meets the blade (you can also clamp it in a machinist's vise and file it). Be sure the blade has been sharpened before you do this. What shows as a tight fit on the unsharpened blade may show a noticeable gap after sharpening.

When you've done this correctly, you can sight the cap-iron/blade assembly against a light and no light will show through. If you can do this in an hour, you're very good. Achieving this snug cap-iron-to-blade fit will help the plane performance considerably. This is about all you can do for a plane like this.

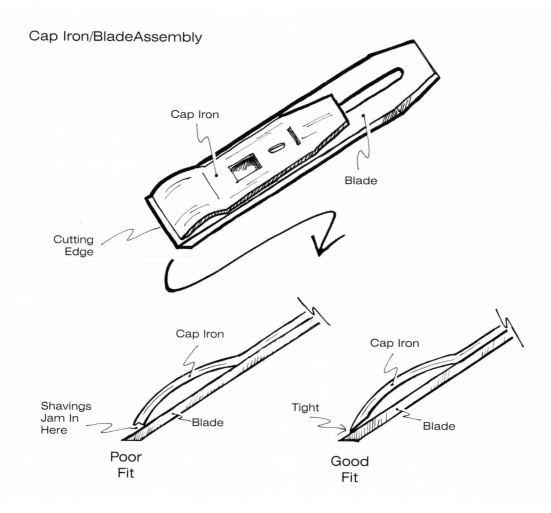

5–4. ◆ *The cap iron on standard-quality planes must be "stoned" to obtain a tight fit to the blade. The cap iron doesn't really do much other than keep the blade rigid.*

"Seating" is also a huge factor in how well a plane works. In any plane, the tighter the "plane iron" (cap-iron/blade assembly) seats on the "frog" (the little ramp), and the tighter the frog seats on the plane body, the better the tool will work (**5–5**). Without tight seating, the parts vibrate against each other and the plane "chatters" over even slightly difficult grain. On high-quality planes, the seating is good. On poor or standard-grade ones, it's not so good.

5–5. ◆ *Finger points to the "frog." Since the frog supports the blade assembly, precise machining is required to "seat" it to the plane body (and to the blade assembly); if not, the plane will "chatter," or vibrate, over the workpiece.*

Can you fix poor seating? Yes. You need to coat one of the mating surfaces with "machinist's blueing" (a thick blue ink), put them together, take them apart, and then grind or file away the high spots. This is repeated over and over and over until there are no more high spots. Sound arduous and time-consuming? It is. You would be ill-advised to even attempt it.

The sole of the plane should be flat also or you won't be able to take a very fine shaving with it. Wood-plane bodies can be flattened on a motorized jointer. To do this, back the iron out from the mouth ¼ inch, but keep it tight in the plane; you want the same tension in the wooden plane body as when you're using it. Use the jointer to take off shavings from the sole ¹⁄₆₄ inch at a time until it's flat. Of course, the jointer must be tuned properly too!

You'll read suggestions saying you can flatten a metal-soled plane yourself, but never by anyone who has ever tried it. I would take it to a machine shop that has a "Blanchard"-type grinder and have them do it. Unless your favorite uncle owns the machine shop, this will cost you more to do than the plane is worth.

From the foregoing, it should be obvious why the so-called "expensive" and "high-priced" planes are really very good bargains. If you have a standard-grade plane, sharpen the blade, fit the cap iron tightly against the blade, and use the plane like that. Accept the fact that its performance will be limited: it will chatter on knotty grain, and shavings will only get so thin. Trying to improve it further simply isn't worth it.

LOW-ANGLE JACK PLANE

To know how a plane should operate, you should get used to a fine-quality plane*. Then you'll have a standard to judge everything else by. The Lie-Nielsen low-angle jack plane is a versatile tool that is simple in

---

*For the procedures described in this chapter, you'll need a scrub plane for roughing out and a jack plane (14 inches long) for smoothing and trueing. Ordinarily a 23-inch jointer plane is also required when planing stock by hand, but we are using only a three-foot board.

design and capable of superior work (**5–6**). If you become thoroughly familiar with this plane, using it exclusively for a year, you will know just how a plane should work and the type of work it can do.

This jack plane is 14 inches long and is capable of surfacing and jointing boards up to about 3 feet long. The sole is flat, so you can take very thin shavings with it (and avoid having to spend time and money flattening it). It has an adjustable throat, so in less than a minute you can open it wider and set the blade to take a deeper cut for rough work, and then reset the throat so it is very narrow and back the blade up for an ultra-thin shaving. The blade is mercifully without a cap iron (so you don't need to file, stone, reset, bend, etc., the cap iron). Its biggest advantage is that the blade is set at a 12-degree angle (**5–7**), allowing it to plane difficult grain and stubborn woods that no other plane can.

The plane comes ready to go: all that is needed to start using it is some honing on the cutting edge. It does what planes should do—

5–6. ◆ *A low-angle jack plane taking shavings from a cherry board with wild grain. Use of this plane for an extended time will teach you how a metal plane should behave.*

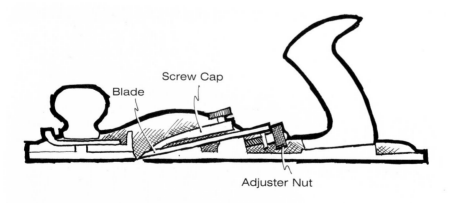

Blade

Screw Cap

Adjuster Nut

Low-Angle Jack Plane Cutaway

5–7. ◆ *This low-angle jack plane has a minimum of parts and is precisely machined. It can plane difficult woods easily and be adjusted in seconds to take a thick or a whisper-thin saving. The blade is massive, so it needs no cap iron.*

shave wood easily, efficiently, and pleasantly! You can learn more from using it for a year than going to a woodworking school or reading 10,000 magazine articles. To find out how to plane wood, you plane wood. You don't follow questionable advice or dabble with inferior tools (imagine Tage Frid or Frank Klaus with a 39-dollar hand plane!).

SCRUB PLANE

The scrub plane (5–8) flattens the board. To get the board flat—not just surfaced or smooth, but *flat*—you need to have a scrub plane. Countless times I have seen students struggle to surface wood with only a jack plane or try to convert an old, smooth plane into a scrub plane. They then spend time trying to flatten a board with it, and it doesn't work. The rough surface will get planed off, and the pretty grain will show as it does on a freshly planed plank, but the board will stay stubbornly unflat. They then try a real scrub plane, and get the board flat in about three minutes.

A scrub plane has a very simple design, as shown in 5–9. It consists of a body, a blade, and a wedge or lever cap to hold the blade down. The blade on a scrub plane is notice-

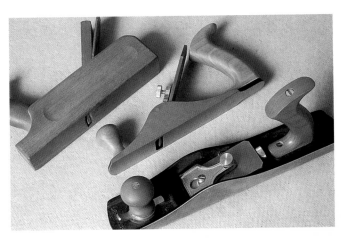

5–8. ◆ *Top and center: scrub planes. Bottom: a low-angle jack plane.*

5–9. ◆ *A metal scrub plane. This plane is utterly simple and does only one thing: scoop out big chunk-like shavings from areas of boards to flatten them. Please don't take your old smooth plane and try to make a scrub plane out of it. Remember the car that could go in water too?—it wasn't much of a car and it was a terrible boat!*

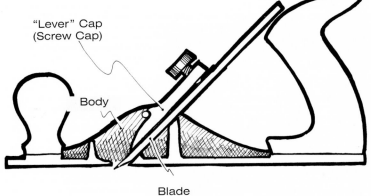

"Lever" Cap
(Screw Cap)

Body

Blade

Scrub Plane

ably rounded (**5–10**). It acts more as a gouge—it scoops. The Lie-Nielsen scrub plane will perform better if the blade is ground to a smaller radius, similar to the radius of an E.C.E. plane blade-about 2¼ inches* (**5–11**). (Should you also slightly grind a radius on blades for jack and smooth planes, like it says in some books and magazine articles? No. There is no noticeable advantage in doing so.)

5–11. ◆ *A Lie-Nielsen scrub-plane blade as it comes from the manufacturer (top) and ground to a 2¼-inch radius (bottom). The blade with the more narrow radius will cut faster and with less effort.*

5–10. ◆ *The sole of a scrub plane. A scrub plane's blade is rounded to remove wood fast.*

FLATTENING A BOARD

Take a piece of rough-sawn hardwood board—oak, cherry, poplar, etc.—about 6 inches wide and 1 inch thick. (Buy it at a lumberyard or hardwood supplier, not a home center.) Cut off a 3-foot section and, placing it on the workbench, try to rock it

from opposite corners. You'll find that it will rock in both directions because it's not flat.

Flip the board over and clamp it to the bench. Adjust the scrub-plane blade so that less than ⅛ inch sticks out the bottom. Plane the board diagonally, first in one direction, and then the other (for example, first from left to right, and then right to left, as indicated in **5–12**). You'll notice how easily and well the scrub plane works (**5–13**), despite the fact that you're removing big chunks of wood.

Flip the board over and, pushing down on opposite corners, try to rock it again (**5–14**). You'll find it doesn't rock at all, or the amount it does is noticeably less. If it does still rock, bring your fingers in from the corners, diagonally, until the board doesn't rock anymore. In between your fingers is a high spot (**5–15**). Make a mental note of where it is. Then flip the board over and plane it out. Two or three times doing this will get one face of the board flat—not surfaced or smooth yet, but flat. Flatness occurs when the face of the board doesn't rock on the bench.

---

* When you hone the scrub-plane blade, you *roll* it on the stone so that the entire microbevel is sharpened. When stropping it, you also roll the edge as you pull it toward you. The back is honed the same way as a regular plane blade, which is discussed in Chapter Four. (To grind the new radius, mark it on the back, grind to the line at 90 degrees to the wheel, and then grind the 25-degree bevel as before. You have to continually rotate the blade as you do this. Dip it in water often.)

5–12. ◆ *Scrub-planing. Go diagonally down the board in one direction, and then from the other.*

5–13. ◆ *The rounded scrub-plane blade leaves ridges in the board. These will be removed with a jack plane.*

5–14. ◆ *Rocking the board to check for flatness. Unless the board is very long, doing this on a flat workbench will tell you if it's flat or not.*

5–15. ◆ *If the board still rocks after scrub planing, move your fingers in until it stops rocking. In between them is a high spot.*

Note: "Flat" is a relative term. The board should be reasonably flat. Reasonably flat means it's flat enough to be part of a table-top or drawer front, etc. "Perfectly" flat is a meaningless term you'll read in some wood-working literature and hear on television shows, as though wood should behave like machined cast iron or granite. Wood looks and feels so wonderful because it's organic, lifelike (leave it overnight in a damp room and it will *move*). You can't make it perfectly flat. Don't make things difficult (impossible!) for yourself.

SURFACING

With the jack plane set for a "thicker" shaving (not tissue-paper thin)*, plane the board diagonally, as before (**5–16**). What's important in this step is not to make the board *unflat*, which is easy to do. Be especially aware

* If you're using any plane besides the Lie-Nielson, this may be the only type of shaving it will make.

5–16. ◆ *With the jack plane set for a slightly thick shaving, the diagonal planing motion is repeated to remove the scrub-plane ridges (but not to unflatten the board!).*

at the corners. When you start the plane stroke, bear down at the front of the plane; as you finish the stroke, bear down at the rear of the plane (**5–17**). Use less pressure at the corners of the board if necessary. If you round them over, you'll unflatten the board. Con-

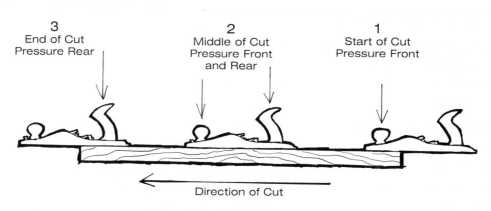

3
End of Cut
Pressure Rear

2
Middle of Cut
Pressure Front
and Rear

1
Start of Cut
Pressure Front

Direction of Cut

Planning Motion/Pressure

5–17. ◆ *Planing motion. To avoid rounding over the edges of your work, use pressure on the front knob at the start of the motion, equal pressure on the front and rear in the middle, and pressure on just the rear as you finish.*

tinue these steps until most of the scrub-plane marks are gone.

Next, set the plane for a thin shaving and plane the board in the direction of the grain (**5–18**). Do this until the board is bright and smoothly surfaced—easy to do if you have the right plane. Again, watch the corners and the ends. When you're finished, flip the board over and check it again for flatness. If it is flat, that side is done (**5–19**).

Surfacing the Other Side

Next, we have to surface the other side. Take a Japanese marking gauge and set it to mark one line at ¾ inch (with the dual-beam design, offset the beams; with the other type, just use one blade). Bearing the fence of the gauge on the side you've just completed, mark the edge all the way around the board (**5–20**). You'll notice how

5–18. ◆ *Finally, with the low-angle jack plane set for a very fine shaving, the board is planed with the grain.*

5–19. ◆ *When finished, the board lies even with the benchtop. It's flat.*

5–20. ◆ *Bearing the fence of the marking gauge against the now flat face of the board, mark the edge for final thickness.*

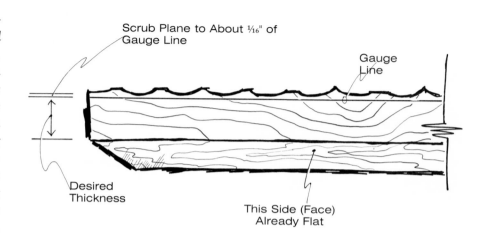

5–21. ◆ *When flattening the second "face" of a board, scrub-plane to within ¹⁄₁₆ inch of the gauge line. Removing the humps with the jack plane (thick-shaving setting) and then surfacing it with the jack plane (thin-shaving setting) will get the thickness to the line.*

Scrub Plane to About ¹⁄₁₆" of Gauge Line

Gauge Line

Desired Thickness

This Side (Face) Already Flat

uneven the amounts of wood are remaining above the line.

With the board clamped again to the bench and the second (rough) side facing up, use the scrub plane and plane the board down to less than ¹⁄₁₆ inch from the gauge line (**5–21**). You don't need to test it by rocking, because it will be parallel to the first side. Finish as before with the jack plane. This should take you down to the gauge line. Both board faces are now flat, surfaced, and parallel to each other.

EDGE-JOINTING

To edge-joint two boards*, clamp them in the bench vise with the edges to be joined facing up. With the jack plane set for a bit more than the thinnest shaving it can make, plane both of the boards at the same time (**5–22**). Keep the plane at 90 degrees to the face of the boards. If you're off a little, the

angles will offset since you are planing both boards together. Use the same precaution at the ends as you did with the corners earlier— it's easy to round them over.

When both edges are planed smooth (and flat), skew the plane body as shown in **5–22** and remove several very thin shavings from

5–22. ◆ *To edge-joint two boards, clamp them together and plane them both at the same time.*

---

*Assumes a 36-inch or shorter board. A longer board will require a jointer plane.

the center two-thirds of the boards. When you unclamp them and hold them together, there should be a *very slight* gap in the center of the boards—about ¹⁄₆₄th of an inch or less (**5–23**). The ends will be tight (**5–24**).

When you glue and clamp the boards together (edge-join them), the clamp pressure will pull the boards tight; when the glue is dry, they will stay tight. We leave the slight gap because the ends of the board will dry out faster than the centers—sometimes they will separate. The gap in the middle insures that the boards will stay tight. This is called "springing the joint" (almost impossible to do precisely with a machine!).

At this point, you have achieved a superior method for preparing stock with hand planes. With the right tools, it really doesn't take much time or effort to do. Of course, machines still have their place. You wouldn't want to prepare all the boards for 24 restaurant tables by hand. But you now know when a board is really flat, and it's important to have the skill to flatten it by hand. And sometimes you'll *need* to know it—there are some boards a machine can't flatten or edge-join.

¹⁄₆₄" **to** ¹⁄₃₂"

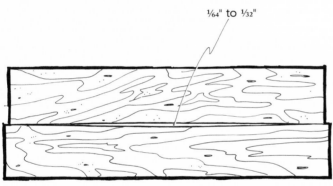

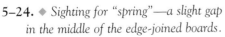

A "Sprung" Joint

5–23. ◆ *A "sprung" edge joint. The ends of boards always dry faster than the middle in a normal climate cycle. A sprung joint insures that the ends will not separate.*

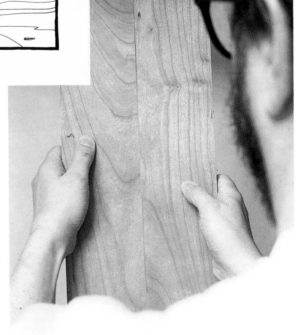

5–24. ◆ *Sighting for "spring"—a slight gap in the middle of the edge-joined boards.*

MAKING MORTISE
& TENON JOINTS

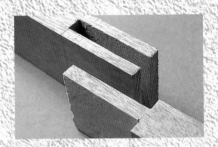

"Good work cannot be produced unless the work is enjoyable; making a thing should bring pleasure, not pain. The work must never be rushed to completion, but done with care and patience."

Hideo Sato, *The Complete Japanese Joinery*

The mortise-and-tenon is said to be the oldest known woodworking joint. It is certainly the most useful, combining great mechanical strength with large glue surfaces. Although it is primarily a frame joint (used on windows, doors, face frames, chairs, tables, etc.), it is the basis for all woodworking joints, including carcass joints (dovetails, tongue-and-groove, spline joints, etc.). Even the highly effective modern biscuit joint is a variation on the mortise-and-tenon joint. It makes sense, therefore, that the first joint to be learned and mastered is the mortise-and-tenon joint.

All joint-making requires the same things: accurate marking and cutting and a good fit. The fit can be determined by some experience—too loose, it won't hold; too tight and the mortise piece will crack. It is a good idea to make your first mortise-and-tenon joints out of fir, mahogany, or poplar because they are a trifle more forgiving than harder woods.

Some people have expressed disbelief regarding a woodworker's ability to make other joints once the mortise-and-tenon is mastered. This is not surprising, since most joint-making instruction in books and elsewhere is so overcomplicated. All woodworking joints are variations on one idea: maximum glue area and mechanical strength. And joint-making is itself a matter of handling tools properly and knowing how the parts should fit—not endless redundancy on thousands of individual details. Learn, really learn, to make a mortise-and-tenon joint well and you'll easily be able to make any other joint.

We will make two joints: a *bridle* (or *slip*) joint (which is an open mortise-and-tenon joint) and the *housed* mortise-and-tenon, where the mortise is a square hole and the joint is hidden (**6–1**).

BRIDLE JOINT

The bridle joint is one of my favorite woodworking joints. It actually has more glue surface than a hidden (housed) mortise-and-tenon joint, and has the wonderful look of hand craftsmanship.

Use 2-inch-wide pieces that are ¾ inch thick. First, mark the board on the face. If you are making a picture, face, or door frame, etc., you can mark with pyramids* (refer to **6–24**). Mark all the way around the ends of each piece (the faces and both edges) with a knife. You mark two inches from the ends because that is the width of each piece (**6–2**); the pieces fit into each other. On one of the pieces (which will be the tenon piece), make a V-cut on each face.

Next, mark for the mortise and tenon. Mark the center of each edge and measure out from there ⅛ inch in each direction (**6–3**). Set the blades of the marking gauge to the two marks on either side of center.

*The pyramids insure that you know which pieces are used for the front of the piece, the back, etc.

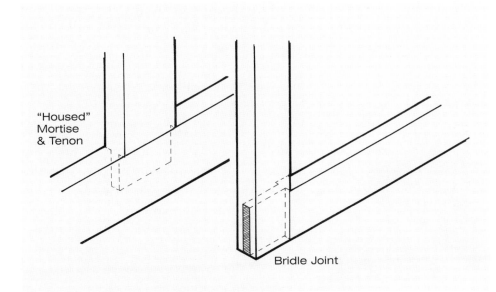

6–1. ◆ *Left: A "housed" (hidden) mortise-and-tenon joint. Right: A bridle joint, which is an "open" mortise-and-tenon joint. The mortise is the hole; the tenon is the part that goes into it.*

"Housed" Mortise & Tenon

Bridle Joint

6–2. ◆ *Marking the ends of the pieces for a bridle joint. These marks define the joint and equal the width of the joining piece.*

6–3. ◆ *Marking the center of the edge, and then ⅛ inch out each way. The mortise gauge is set to these outer marks.*

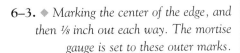

Now, use the gauge to draw a line from the original knife mark, up the edge across the end grain, and down the other edge on the other side (**6–4**). Repeat this on the other piece. Be sure you index to the same face side again (the side with the pyramid marks on it).

6–4. ◆ *Marking for the mortise-and-tenon pieces. The Japanese gauge makes it easy to mark clear, accurate lines.*

What you have now are two identically marked pieces. The centerpiece of one will stay there and be the tenon; the centerpiece of the other will be cut out and be the mortise. Mark with an "X" the waste areas (**6–5**). To make them fit well, they must be sawn accurately. The key to doing that is to saw on the waste side of the line for the tenon cut (that is, to saw to the *outside* of the line) and to saw to the inside of the line for the mortise cut.

In any mortise-and-tenon joint, the mortise (hole) is always made first. The tenon is then cut to fit the mortise, and can be adjusted easily if the fit is off, which it very often is. Television woodworkers and book and magazine writers who show three quick steps and then a perfectly fitting tenon are showing you utter fantasy. By hand or by machine, tenons almost always need to be trimmed to fit right.

Marking Waste Areas For Bridle Joint

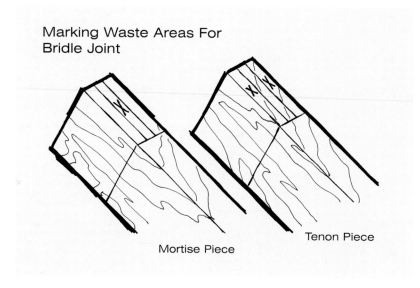

Mortise Piece   Tenon Piece

6–5. ◆ *Marking bridle-joint waste areas. The "X" indicates the areas that are cut out. Don't leave this step out or you'll end up with two tenon or mortise pieces. You will concentrate so hard on cutting accurately, you'll forget what to cut!*

First the mortise. Clamp the workpiece in the vise diagonally, facing away from you. Using a nine-point bow saw, place its blade on the inside of one of the cutting lines, using the knuckle of your thumb as a guide. Draw the saw back toward you to begin making a saw kerf. This is an important step. If the cut doesn't get started correctly, it won't be accurate. Saw from the corner down until you reach the gauge line (**6–6**). Repeat with the other line. Stay on the *inside* of the line (for the mortise piece).

Unclamp the board and turn it around in the vise, this time facing straight up. Place the saw in the previously cut kerf and again saw down to the gauge line. With the saw lying loosely in your hand, this is easy to do. The saw blade will follow the previously cut kerf (**6–7**). If it begins to stray off line a bit, the bow saw will allow you to coax it back on track. Be sure not to saw beyond the line; check the other side too as you get to the finish point.

When the sawing has been completed, the center waste is then chopped out with a chisel. Clamp the workpiece on the bench and use a ¼-inch chisel and mallet or hammer to chop downward from the line (**6–8**). Chop downward about ⅜ inch*; then pull the chisel out. Chop out some waste to the side of your vertical chisel cut in a V shape, as shown in **6–9**.

The bridle-joint tenon is sawn the same way as the mortise, except that the saw cuts to the *outside* of the line and there are "shoulder" cuts. The shoulder cuts are crosscuts from the original knife-line V-cuts down

*You are also chopping inward a few degrees, undercutting a little to insure a tight fit later (you are cutting end grain here, which isn't a glue surface anyway).

6–6. ◆ *Sawing to the line with a 9-point bow saw (German). Clamping the piece at an angle helps to begin the joint-cutting.*

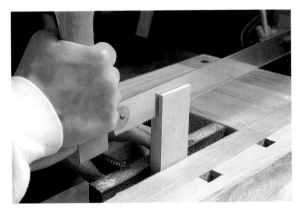

6–7. ◆ *Finishing the cut with the piece straight up in the vise. With the proper grip on the saw (loose), the blade will follow the kerf easily.*

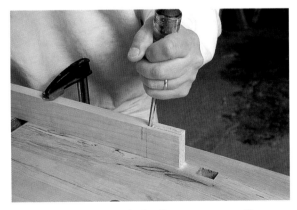

6–8. ◆ *Chopping out the bridle-joint mortise. Here, I'm just beginning, and you can see the chisel angled slightly for the undercutting in the end grain.*

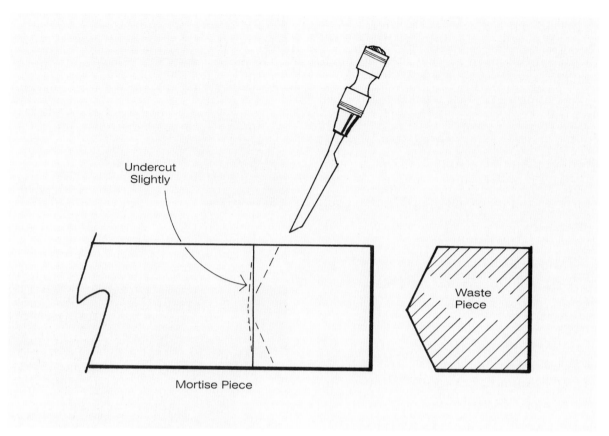

Undercut
Slightly

Waste
Piece

Mortise Piece

6–9. ◆ *The bridle-joint mortise. The undercut insures that the tenon piece will fit tight.*

6–10. ◆ *Cutting the tenon shoulders. Since the material I'm removing is about ¼ inch thick, the small saw works well.*

to the cheek cuts (you can do the shoulder cuts before the cheek cuts if you like). I lay the piece against the bench stop and cut it with an offset dovetail saw (**6–10**). You can also use a bow saw in a bench hook to do this. With the waste removed, clean out the corners with a chisel if necessary. That completes the tenon.

Test the fit of the tenon and the mortise. If it's too tight, you can shave the tenon *cheeks* a bit with a 1-inch rabbet or shoulder plane (**6–11 to 6–13**). (A rasp will also work.) A rabbet plane is a skinny plane that can work right up against an edge. Trim the cheek a bit at a time, checking the fit of the mortise and tenon as you go. If the fit is too

6–11. ◆ *Using a shoulder plane to trim the tenon cheeks (the wide parts) for a good fit.*

6–12. ◆ *Fitting the pieces. There should be just a slight resistance as you slip the joint together; the pieces should not fit too loosely or tightly.*

6–13. ◆ *The finished bridle joint.*

loose, you can glue pieces of veneer to the tenon cheeks, and then fit the pieces as before. If the shoulders don't fit tight into the mortise piece, the shoulder plane can trim them as well.

"HOUSED" MORTISE-AND-TENON JOINT

For this mortise-and-tenon joint, which is hidden, the tenon is cut just as for the bridle joint, with two shoulders. Some believe that the tenon should have four shoulders in order to hide the joint (**6–14***). This is not only a more difficult joint to cut (all shoulders must be in the same plane), it doesn't

*Illus. **6–14** shows a "housed" mortise-and-tenon joint in the middle of a workpiece. For the same joint on the end of a board, you would use a "haunch" or three-shoulder tenon, etc.

possess the same amount of glue surface as a two-shoulder tenon.

For this joint, use stock that is 3 inches wide × 1 inch thick. Mark the faces. The mortise will be a bit more than ¼ inch wide. You'll need a bit brace and a ¼-inch auger bit (**6–15** and **6–16**). Most of the hole is bored out with the auger bit; the sides and ends are squared up with a chisel. Using an auger bit in a bit brace teaches you to line up and bore a hole straight and square. The bit, being long, is easy to align; the motion of the brace is slow and it is easy to keep the brace steady. If, like most people, you go directly to a power drill, you'll drill the holes crooked.

Again, you make the mortise first. In this case, mark out the width of the tenon piece, which is 3 inches. Next, mark the center of the mortise with a line from end to end. The result will be an "I" shape (**6–17**). Mark in from the edges ⅜ inch.

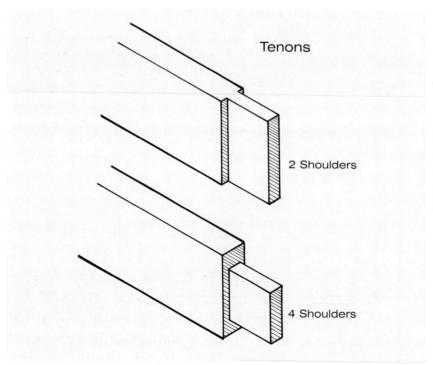

Tenons

2 Shoulders

4 Shoulders

6–14. ◆ *The two-shoulder mortise-and-tenon joint not only has more glue surface than the four-shoulder type, it's also easier to cut.*

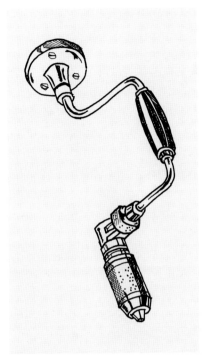

6–15. ◆ *A bit brace. Most models like this can be set to forward- or reverse-crank, and also to ratchet.*

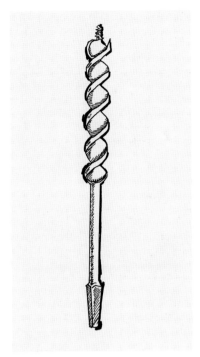

6–16. ◆ *An auger bit. The screw tip on this long bit pulls the cutters into the work.*

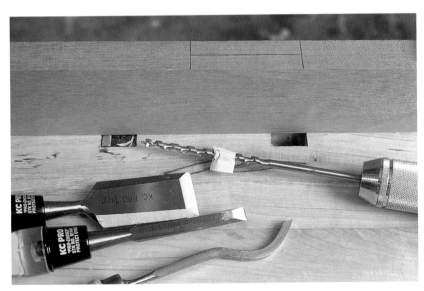

6–17. ◆ *As shown in the background, the edges and the center of the mortise have been marked. Note the crank-neck chisel in the foreground; it is useful, but not essential, for cleaning out the bottoms of housed mortises.*

Place the center screw of the auger bit on this mark. Drill (actually "bore") down 1½ inches in both spots (a piece of masking tape on the bit shows you where to stop).

Boring straight holes with a brace and bit is easy if you line the work up. Clamp the mortise piece straight up on the bench. Place the center screw on the mark and align the assembly straight with the workpiece. Leaving your hand on top of the brace, bring your head to the side to align it 90 degrees to the workpiece (6–18). Don't be too meticulous

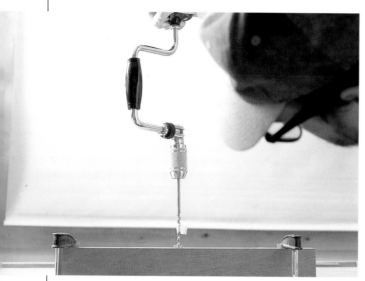

6–18. ◆ *Aligning the brace and bit with the work. After a while, boring straight, square holes with this tool becomes a matter of "feel."*

here—get the tool to where it looks and feels right and start boring the holes. If you're off a little, it's okay. What's important is to get the proper *feel* of the correct position. In time, it will come automatically. (With a power hand drill, the pistol configuration prevents you from lining anything up; with a drill press, the machine aligns it for you. In either case, you learn nothing.)

When the two outside holes are bored, bore holes in between them to clear out the majority of the waste (**6–19**). Don't overlap the holes, because the bit may have a tendency to drift, although the screw usually will keep it on line. Once the holes are bored, the mortise is squared up with chisels.

With the mortise gauge indexed to the face side (the side with the pyramids), set the blades to about 1/16 inch on either side of the holes. Lock them in place and draw them across the work, from end line to end line. The width will be around 3/8 inch (**6–20**). The gauge lines you just drew indicate the *sides* of the mortise. Leave the gauge at this setting.

With a 1/4-inch chisel, chop the *ends* of the mortise square. Chop down a bit (don't un-

6–19. ◆ *Boring out the waste. The masking tape on the auger bit is a depth gauge; when it sweeps away the wood chips, the hole is deep enough.*

dercut), and then clear out a bit of waste as you did with the bridle-joint mortise. Do this until you reach the bottom. You are chopping end grain, so you can tap the chisel lightly with a mallet. Next, take a wide chisel and shave the sides of the mortise (**6–21**). Use hand pressure; *it's very easy to crack the piece.*

Take thin shavings, keeping the chisel square to the sides of the work. When the cutting line is equal to the gauge line, you're finished. It's very important to use very light pressure since you're cutting with the grain. As you chop and trim with the chisel, remove waste from the mortise (**6–22**).

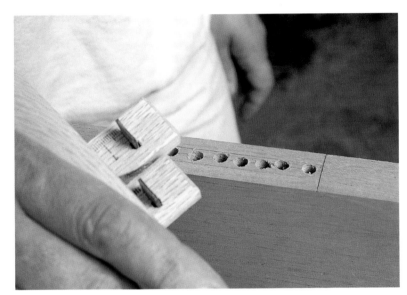

6–20. ◆ *Lines marked with a gauge for the mortise sides.*

6–21. ◆ *Cutting the sides of the mortise straight with the chisel (the ends have already been chopped out somewhat).*

6–22. ◆ *Using a narrow chisel to clean out the mortise waste. I am careful not to cut into the ends of the mortise as I do this.*

The tenon is made the same way as for the bridle joint, with a few exceptions. Make the length about ⅛ inch shorter than the depth of the mortise. This is to insure enough clearance in case the bottom of the mortise is uneven. Also be sure to use the previous gauge setting. Otherwise, cut the tenon with the bow saw the same way as before, trimming with a rabbet or shoulder plane as necessary (**6–23**).

MASTERING JOINT-MAKING

Most people never master any area of woodworking, least of all joint-making. One reason for this is that they continue to make the same mistakes. I've seen students consistently try to use the wrong tools and/or methods and create crooked, badly fitting pieces—over and over and over.

It is important to learn how to cut mortise-and-tenon joints because this will teach

6–23. ◆ *Fitting the joint. The "feel" should be the same as for the bridle joint. If it's too tight, the mortise piece will crack.*

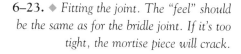

you to recognize *the proper feel* of the mating pieces of a correctly made joint. Will you make them perfectly the first time? Probably not (you should have seen my first one!). You can, however, control how good you can get through plain hard work.

How? Practice. Make five sets of each joint or make several practice frames like the one shown in **6–24**. Using the right tools (the saw especially) will allow you to get better and better with each attempt. Keep a record of your mistakes by writing them down in a notebook, and make a conscious effort to correct each mistake on the next try. If you do this, you'll soon run out of mistakes. Eventually, every mortise-and-tenon joint you make will fit beautifully.

What if a bit of the joint shows? First of all, as long as it's carefully made, no one will care. Second, handwork should *look* hand-made, not manufactured.

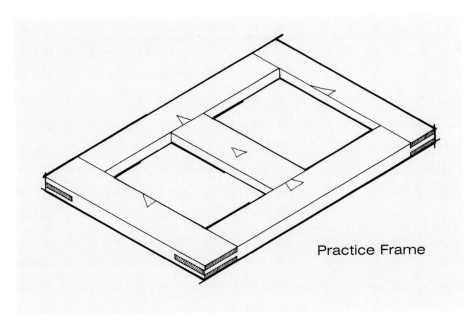

Practice Frame

6–24. ◆ *A practice frame. Build several. First make the pieces 1 inch thick and 2 inches wide. Then make them 3 inches wide. Note the pyramid markings; they indicate what piece is the left side, top, etc. Marking gauges are always indexed to the side with the pyramids.*

Seven

WOOD FINISHING

"You can build a beautiful piece, but if the finish is bad, both beauty and value will be lessened."

Tage Frid, *Tage Frid Teaches Woodworking*, Taunton Press, 1993

Finishing is often a confusing subject for woodworkers to read or learn about. Very often, too many finishing products—and techniques for using them—are discussed. Like other aspects of woodworking, competence is achieved by becoming thoroughly familiar with one product and technique at a time. Then you'll not only have a basis for comparison, you'll also have confidence in one method that works.

Woodworkers often jump from idea to idea, trying a new finish or method every time they do a job. Why? Because manufacturers and woodworkers claim to have a newer, better, faster, easier product/method (this week). Lost in all of this are some fundamental questions: What properties does the finish need to have (for example, should it be waterproof or not)? What is the shop capable of doing? (A lacquer finish may be just right for a certain piece of furniture, but if you don't have room for a spray booth and an air compressor, you can't use it.) And most important: How do you want the wood to look?

Polyurethane varnish is mentioned often in magazines and on woodworking television shows as a good finish. It's waterproof, the water-based material dries fast, and it "protects" the wood. But how does it look? They never tell us that. Polyurethane is a liquid plastic. It encases (embalms?) the wood in plastic. I've used it on commercial jobs, but dislike it. The finish is hard, bright, un-touchable. It makes wood resemble that awful fake wood paneling you see in home centers. Why anyone would want to make such a fine-looking natural material look artificial is beyond me, but people do it.

In this chapter we will cover only two finishes: oil and shellac. Oil is easy to apply, waterproof, and provides a lovely finish. Shellac dries fast and looks beautiful without too much bother. Both finishes are good for dusty shops without a dedicated finishing area.

PREPARING THE WOOD FOR A FINISH

How Well Should the Wood Be Prepared?

My wife and I have a blanket chest that dates from the Revolutionary War (**7-1**). The wood is ink-stained, there are cracks in the top, and the moldings don't line up anymore. These "flaws" actually make it more attractive. There is a handmade character and look to it that is lacking in modern work: you can see and *feel* the craftsman's tool marks on the wood. It isn't the fact that the piece is old that makes it so special. It's special because it shows that someone made it. The flaws in it are inconsequential. The message still gets through.

I have a saying: "Wood should look like wood." This means that excess sanding

7–1. ◆ *Blanket chest built before 1770. The top doesn't fit, it's cracked and ink-stained, the moldings are askew, and the handles on the side are broken off. No matter: it's still beautiful. Excess work on this piece to prepare it for a finish would destroy its character. Only mediocre work needs to be perfect; good work can be considerably flawed.*

and labor to make a piece of wood as smooth and flawless as glass is unnecessary and unwanted. Often, just the smooth plane is enough to prepare the wood for finishing. The tool marks left by a plane are perfectly acceptable—even desirable. They show that a craftsman made the piece, not a machine.

Preparation Technique

Before any finish is applied, the wood must be prepared for finishing. For years I used nothing but a hand plane for this—an old fifteen-dollar garage-sale smooth plane that I coaxed into working. I still use a plane today, but now I use a low-angle smooth plane (**7–2** and **7–3**). It makes very thin shavings (**7–4**)

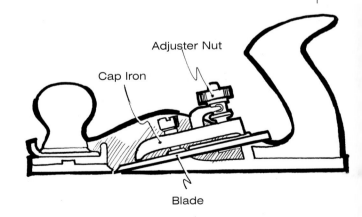

Adjuster Nut

Cap Iron

Blade

Low-Angle Smooth Plane

7–2 and 7–3. ◆ *A low-angle smooth plane—like the jack plane—has few parts. It works especially well on difficult, knotty woods.*

7–4. ◆ *A low-angle smooth plane can be used for surface preparation. The low-angle design makes it possible to plane even a difficult surface. Note the thin shavings that can be produced with this plane.*

and, because it's a high-quality tool, you expend little energy using it. The low-angle blade allows it to plane almost any wood easily (**7–5** and **7–6**).

A #4 bench smooth plane (**7–7**) or a wooden smooth plane (**7–8**) can also be used to prepare the surface for a finish. Another approach is to make and use a sanding block (**7–9** to **7–12**). You use the sanding block with 220-grit sandpaper after planing with the smooth plane. You can also use the block with progressively finer grits of sandpaper (80, 120, 150, and 220) instead of planing. I

7–5. ◆ *Using a low-angle smooth plane to prepare the surface for a finish.*

7–6. ◆ *A smooth plane is used from all angles on the workpiece; hence the importance of a sharp blade and of taking very fine shavings.*

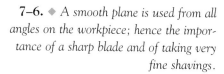

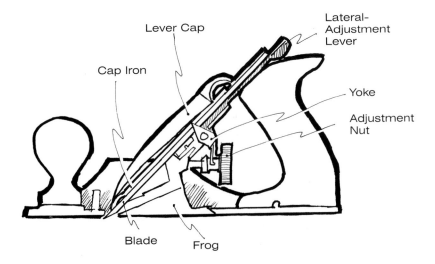

Lever Cap

Cap Iron

Lateral-
Adjustment
Lever

Yoke

Adjustment
Nut

Blade   Frog

Bench Smooth Plane Simplified Cutaway

7–7. ◆ *The #4 bench smooth plane. This plane has more parts than the low-angle smooth plane, but works just as well. Ultra-precise machine fitting is the reason.*

prefer using just the smooth plane; it's faster and lends more character to the piece.

If you dimension boards by hand, as described in Chapter Five, you can leave them as they are when they're flattened. They'll have the wonderful character of the blanket chest described previously. When you buy wood that's been machine-surfaced, you'll need to remove all the planer marks with the smooth plane. Isn't it interesting that hand tools leave a naturally pretty surface and machines leave an ugly one?

Once the surface has been prepared, it's time to add the finish. Below I describe finishing techniques for oil and shellac finishes.

7–8. ◆ *Wooden smooth plane. This is a good, general-purpose smooth plane.*

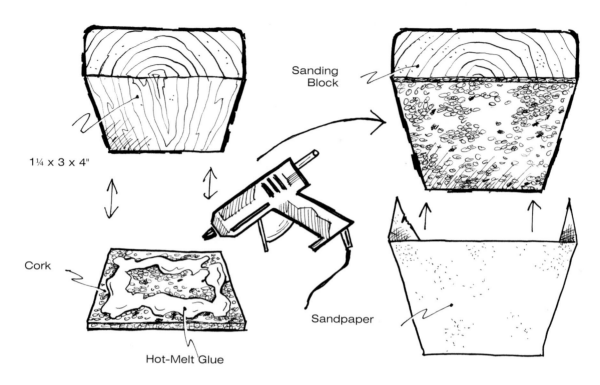

1¼ x 3 x 4"

Cork

Hot-Melt Glue

Sanding
Block

Sandpaper

Making a Sanding Block

7–9. ◆ *A sanding block can be easily made by gluing cork material to the bottom of a scrap of pine. It works much better than the rubber ones sold in paint stores.*

7–10. ◆ *A view of the sanding block showing the cork "sole." Cork provides a firm platen for the sandpaper, but also "gives" a bit.*

7–11. ◆ *The sanding block ready for use. Why sand when you've already smooth-planed the wood? Because sandpaper can reach spots the plane sometimes cannot, and prepares the wood to receive the finish. Most woodworkers sand too much.*

Sanding Motion

Sanding Block

Sand with the Grain. "Double Up" on the Ends

7–12. ◆ *"Double up" on the ends of a stroke whenever you sand (that is, go over the ends twice). It provides a more even sanding job.*

OIL FINISHES

An oil finish (**7–13**) is really the ideal finish for wood. It gives it a beautiful depth and character. An oil finish is a penetrating finish—it actually soaks *into* the wood. In addition to looking the nicest, it's the easiest finish to apply: you wipe it on, let in soak in for awhile, and then wipe it off again. You don't need to be concerned with dust settling on the pieces and ruining the finish (a concern for many small shops), or brush marks, drips, etc.

Below I describe finishing techniques for linseed, Danish, and tung-oil finishes.

7–13. ◆ *All of these penetrating oil finishes will do a fine job on furniture. An oil finish gives the wood a plain, natural look.*

Linseed-Oil Finish

Linseed oil is the first oil finish I ever saw. I grew up around that awful, too-glossy, stained (to look like cherry) poplar furniture and was unprepared for the natural look linseed oil gives to wood. For many years, this was the standard oil finish for furnituremakers.

Linseed oil is inexpensive and available in home centers. Be sure to use boiled linseed oil* (as indicated on the can), not raw linseed oil. Raw linseed oil is used for waterproofing outdoor wood and will never dry if used on indoor furniture. *Also, with any oil finish, dispose of the rags outdoors immediately after use.* When I lived in St. Louis, one of my students almost burned his house down ignoring this advice. Luckily, his wife noticed the smoking rags in time.

To get started, mix boiled linseed oil at about a 50-50 ratio with turpentine in a glass jar (**7–14** and **7–15**). Apply this mixture to the workpiece with a rag, using lots of oil (**7–16**). When the entire piece is covered, look to see any dry spots and reapply oil and turpentine there. After about 15 or so minutes of this, stop and let the piece sit for about 20 minutes; then wipe off the excess. Let the piece sit for 24 hours.

For the next coat, use 100-percent boiled linseed oil at room temperature. If you use it at a colder temperature, it won't penetrate well. Apply it the same way as before, using a heavy coat of oil and reapplying oil to the dry spots. Wipe any excess off after 20 minutes. After another 24 hours, apply a third coat the same way. After three applications, the finish is complete. In a day, the piece is dry and ready to use.

Generally for any oil finish, some craftsmen like to apply the second and third coats of oil into the wood with steel wool and/or sand (lightly) with 320-grit sandpaper between coats. I don't bother to do this.

Note: Don't use an oil finish inside draw-

*Boiled linseed oil has dryers added that lessen the curing time of the finish.

7–14. ◆ *Preparing a first-coat linseed-oil finish. First, pour boiled linseed oil into a glass jar.*

7–15. ◆ *Adding turpentine to the linseed oil. About a 50-50 mix of turpentine and oil works well.*

7–16. ◆ *Applying linseed oil with a rag. Use generous amounts of oil—especially for the first coat. Linseed oil darkens the wood more than other oil finishes. Promptly dispose of the rags outside after use.*

ers. It can bleed a bit in hot weather and soil paper and cloth. There's really no reason to finish the inside of drawers anyway.

Tung-Oil Finish

Tung-oil finishes are said to have the most resistance to water, alcohol, acid, etc. Like linseed oil, I use them in a three-day sequence (**7–17** and **7–18**). Repeated applications of tung-oil finish will build up a satiny sheen on the wood. One brand contains wax, which will give a bit of luster to the piece, although tung oil in general will naturally produce a bit more gloss than other oils. The more coats you apply, the glossier the finish. I usually use two or three coats.

Tung oil is my favorite oil finish. It's easy to use and produces the best-looking finish.

Danish Oil

Danish oil is similar to linseed oil, but it's easier to use. If you want to, you can finish a piece in one day. As with linseed oil, the piece is flooded initially with the oil, but you

7–17. ◆ *Tung oil being applied with a brush.*

7–18. ◆ *Removing tung oil with a rag. Once the surface has been flooded for about 30 minutes, excess oil can be wiped off.*

use the oil straight from the can (**7–19**). After covering the piece, wait 30 minutes and then apply another coat of oil. Fifteen minutes after this second application, wipe the piece off. It will be ready for use in about 12 hours.

Danish oil is the easiest (and the most-expensive) oil finish to use. I like it because I can finish a piece quickly.

7–19. ◆ *Applying Danish oil finish to a dovetailed oak box. This box was first finished with orange shellac.*

7–20. ◆ *Orange and super-blonde shellac. The flakes are mixed with denatured alcohol to make a working solution. Orange shellac is good for darker woods, super blonde for lighter woods.*

SHELLAC

There are two types of shellac you're likely to need: orange and blonde (also called super blonde) (**7–20**). Orange shellac gives a warm tone to darker woods like cherry, oak, walnut, fir, etc. Super blonde is good for lighter-colored woods such as ash and hard and soft maple.

The best way to make a shellac finish is to mix your own*. In a glass peanut-butter or spaghetti-sauce jar (never use metal for shellac), put in about two inches of shellac flakes. Pour in enough denatured alcohol to cover the flakes about one inch (**7–21**).

*Freshly mixed shellac will perform much better than the premixed types. Premixed shellac has a retarding agent that gives it an indefinite shelf life in the store. Shellac you mix yourself will last for months once it's mixed, but you should still test a premixed batch before using it. With your finger, dab a bit of it on a piece of glass. Orange shellac should be dry in about one minute (in a 68-degree Fahrenheit room), and super blonde in about two minutes.

7–21. ◆ *Adding denatured alcohol to super-blonde shellac flakes. For a small amount like this, I cover the flakes about ½ inch with the alcohol.*

Shake the jar for one or two minutes continuously to prevent the flakes from clumping (7–22), and then every three or four minutes until all the flakes dissolve. Orange shellac will dissolve faster than super-blonde shellac.

You can apply shellac with either a brush or a rag (7–23). The more coats you apply, the glossier the finish will be. Sand lightly between coats with 220-grit sandpaper to smooth the wood and even out the finish. Unlike oil, shellac can be used inside drawers and carcasses if desired. Dust the piece between coats with a rag and use a tack cloth before the final coat.

Shellac dries so quickly that you can finish an entire piece in one day, so any dust in your shop doesn't have a chance to settle on (and become a part of) the piece. Application is quick and easy, even for beginners. Shellac's disadvantage is that it isn't water- or alcohol-proof or heat-resistant, so it's not a good choice for bar or dining-table tops, etc. It is, however, very easy to repair. Sand the damaged area and reapply the shellac.

7–22. ◆ *Shaking the jar of shellac flakes and alcohol to prevent the flakes from clumping. Shellac should be reasonably fresh when you use it. If in doubt, dab a bit of old shellac on a piece of glass. If it isn't dry in one minute, don't use it; throw it away. It will never dry properly.*

7–23. ◆ *"Padding on" shellac (applying it with a rag). Shellac is a wonderful finish for items that don't need to be waterproof, like this maple and cherry letter box.*

A FINAL WORD ABOUT FINISHING

My first woodworking teacher taught me to use a linseed-oil finish. For my first three years of serious woodworking, that's all I used. I became thoroughly familiar with linseed-oil finish on all types of wood, and I used it later as a basis of comparison for all other finishes I tried. Most didn't measure up, but I wouldn't have known that if I hadn't known what looked right to me.

Many woodworkers accept the advice in magazine and book articles or from people on television without even thinking twice about it. Look at furniture and develop a personal preference. Many museums and art galleries have furniture on display you can view, or you can visit antiques dealers. It's also good to know what to *dislike*—go to a low-end furniture "warehouse" and look at its pieces. You'll see cheesy-looking, ultra-high-gloss veneered particleboard or that awful glossy stained poplar that only gangsters could love.

It isn't important that you like and use what I like and use. What is important is to become well-acquainted with one method that works well. This means experimenting with different techniques. Try samples of oil and shellac finish on different woods to see what they look like. Do you know that you can apply shellac to wood, let it dry, and then oil over it (**7–24**)? Try that, too. See how two, three, six, and ten coats of oil look on different woods. Then try this with shellac also—both orange and blonde. Try it with oil over shellac, as well as oil over raw wood. If you do this, you'll know more when you're done than most wood finishers.

7–24. ◆ *Applying a tung-oil product to a box lid. Any oil finish can be used over a first coat (or coats) of shellac.*

APPENDICES

Glossary

Backsaw A handsaw with a stiffening bar along its back to keep the blade rigid. Most don't cut well.

Bevel The angled area at the cutting edge of a plane blade or chisel.

Biscuit Joint A spline joint made with a biscuit joiner (a dedicated machine) and prefabricated, compressed hardwood plates (biscuits).

Bit Brace A rotary-action hand tool, sometimes ratcheted, most often used with an auger bit, for boring large holes (over ¼ inch). It is also used to drive screws.

Blind Joint Any hidden joint (no elements of the joint or mechanical fasteners are visible).

Blonde Shellac A clear wood shellac finish (as opposed to orange shellac).

Bow Saw A saw, widely used in continental Europe, that holds a blade in tension within a wooden frame. The blade is thin and cannot whip or kink, and so cuts very fast and accurately.

Box Joint An interlocking finger joint, best made by machine, usually seen on small boxes but useful for larger work, too.

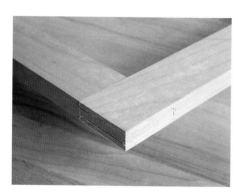

Bridle Joint An open mortise-and-tenon joint.

Burr The small rough bit of metal remaining on a tool edge after grinding.

Butt Joint A joint, usually nailed, in which the edge or end of one board is butted against the face of another board. Most often, it is a poor joint.

Cap Iron A cover piece that screws to a plane blade to hold it rigid.

Carcass The basic box of a cabinet.

Carpenter's Handsaw The panel saw—what most of us think of as a woodworking handsaw. Its blades are thick, cut slowly, and make a large kerf. It is of almost no use.

Combination Square A measuring tool with a head that is designed to lay out 45- and 90-degree angles. The head slides along the blade; this permits it to be used to mark boards to width. The combination square is also used to check for squareness and levelness, and many other things.

Crosscut A cut across the grain of the wood.

Dado Joint A joint often used in making shelves, in which the horizontal piece is housed in the dado (groove) cut into the vertical piece. It should always be shouldered.

Danish Oil A penetrating oil finish.

Diamond Stones Extremely hard sharpening stones that consist of microscopic, industrial diamond crystals bonded to a flat matrix.

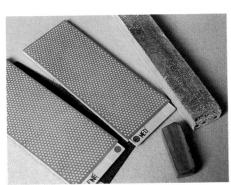

Dividers Measuring tools used to lay out circles and to transfer measurements. They have two sharp, pointed metal legs.

Dovetail Joint A strong two-part joint that consists of a tail and a mating pin. Often used in drawers.

Dovetail Saw In America, usually this refers to a small handsaw with a turned handle. A 9-point bow saw is truly the ideal dovetail (joint-making) saw.

"Dressing" Grinder Wheels Using a grinder wheel dresser to clean the wheel of metal particles and keep the face of it flat.

Edge Jointing Making the edges of boards straight and square, in order to glue them together.

End Grain Exposed open cells on the ends of a board. Not a glue surface.

Folding Rule A rigid measuring ruler that folds for storage.

Fore Plane A plane approximately 18 inches long.

Grain Direction The orientation of the fibers in wood.

Green Wood Unseasoned lumber, referred to as "wet."

Grinding A process in sharpening a tool that obtains a fresh bevel. The next step in the process is honing, which makes the blade razor-sharp.

Half-Lap Joint A simple, shouldered woodworking joint.

High Spots Areas on the face of a board that are higher than the surround.

Hollow-Ground Bevel A curved bevel made with a grinding wheel, as opposed to a bevel made on a flat sharpening stone.

Honing A process in sharpening blades that makes a rough-ground blade razor-sharp.

Jack Plane A general-purpose hand plane that is approximately 12 to 17 inches long.

Jointer Plane A 23- to 24-inch plane that will obtain a flat surface on the longest boards, whether on an edge or the face.

Jointing Making an edge straight and square with the face of the board.

Linseed-Oil Finish A simple, penetrating oil finish.

Marking Gauge A tool used to lay out lines parallel to the edges on a board. The best type have a Japanese design that uses a blade for marking.

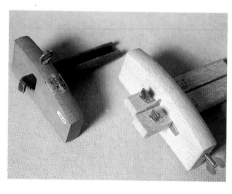

Marking Knife A sharp knife used to mark out joinery or dimensioning cuts.

Microbevel A small, secondary bevel at the very edge of a larger bevel, usually on a chisel or a plane blade.

Miter Joint A joint made by fastening pieces together at a 45-degree angle.

Mortise Gauge Similar to a marking gauge, a tool with a fence and two beams that is used to mark mortises and tenons, and can also be used to make other markings.

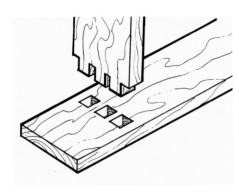

Mortise-and-Tenon Joint A very strong joint in which the mortise (hole) is cut into one piece and the tenon (mating piece) fits into the slot. The essential woodworking joint.

Needle Files Very small files used for sharpening tiny saw teeth.

Oil Finish A waterproof finish that penetrates the wood and allows a natural patina. The wood still looks like wood.

Orange Shellac A less-refined grade of shellac than blonde that still retains some of the orange color.

Points per Inch Number of teeth there are per inch in a saw blade.

PVA (Polyvinyl Acetate) Glue Twenty-dollar term for modern yellow or white glues. They are nontoxic, inexpensive, clean up easily with water, and have strong bonding qualities.

Rabbet Joint An L-shaped channel that goes along the edge of a piece of stock.

Rabbet Plane Skinny plane used to cut rabbets, trim tenons, etc.

Rip Cut A cut made with the grain of the wood.

Saw Set A tool that is used to set the teeth of a saw blade.

Scrub Plane A plane with a rounded blade that scoops rather than shaves, and is used to *initially* flatten boards. These planes remove wood fast.

Set The amount that saw teeth are offset from each other.

Shellac A finish material made from lac—a resin produced by small insects.

Shoulder The "buttress" of any good woodworking joint. It creates mechanical strength by minimizing or eliminating "racking," in which a joint comes out of square on all four corners.

Sliding Dovetail A dovetail-shaped dado joint, very useful in carcass construction, that is glued on one end. An unusual mixture of great strength and allowance for wood movement.

Slip Joint *See* Bridle Joint.

Springing a Joint A technique that involves leaving a gap in the center of two edge-joined boards to insure that the boards—particularly the ends—will stay tight.

Square Parts that are at right (90-degree) angles to each other; also, a box or frame in the condition of having all four corners at 90 degrees.

Standard-Grade Plane Generally, this means a tool of lesser quality—not machined to high tolerances, not finished well, blades made with poor-quality steel, etc.

Storypole A shop-made stick with dimensions marked on it. This allows dimensions to be made directly from a piece of furniture, a room, or plans to the stick; then the dimensions are transferred to the workpieces via the pole. It is more accurate than measuring.

Strop A piece of thick leather, tacked "flesh side" out to a hardwood block, that is used with a compound to hone a blade.

Tongue-and-Groove Joint An edge dado joint, often used in flooring and decking materials.

Tung Oil A natural oil derived from the seeds of tung trees. It is used by itself or mixed with other oils to make penetrating oil finishes.

Tuning Adjusting all of the working parts of a plane to their theoretically optimum positions. Usually an excuse for wasting time.

Turpentine A solvent used in oil-based finishes. It is considered the ideal thinner for linseed oil.

Utility Knife A heavy-duty knife with a replaceable, often retractable, blade.

Water Stone Usually a man-made or natural stone used to sharpen blades. It is used with water.

Whetstone An abrasive stone (usually an oilstone) used to sharpen blades. Also called an Arkansas stone. Used with oil, usually kerosene.

White Glue PVA glue. It has a longer drying time and is more "rubbery" than yellow glue. Either is fine.

White or Super-Blonde Shellac The most highly re-fined grade of shellac. It is bleached to remove all of the orange color of the raw shellac.

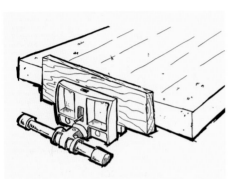

Woodworking Bench Vise The part of the bench used to hold boards. Depending on the vise used, the boards can be held on edge, end up, or flat on the bench top.

Yellow Glue PVA (polyvinyl acetate) glue. It sets faster and is more brittle than white PVA glue (so as to sand easier).

Index

Metric Conversion Chart

INCHES TO MILLEMETERS AND CENTIMETERS
MM— Millemeters   CM—Centimeters

Inches	MM	CM	Inches	CM	Inches	CM
⅛	3	0.3	9	22.9	30	76.2
¼	6	0.6	10	25.4	31	78.7
⅜	10	1.0	11	27.9	32	81.3
½	13	1.3	12	30.5	33	83.8
⅝	16	1.6	13	33.0	34	86.4
¾	19	1.9	14	35.6	35	88.9
⅞	22	2.2	15	38.1	36	91.4
1	25	2.5	16	40.6	37	94.0
1¼	32	3.2	17	43.2	38	96.5
1½	38	3.8	18	45.7	39	99.1
1¾	44	4.4	19	48.3	48	101.6
2	51	5.1	20	50.8	41	104.1
2½	64	6.4	21	53.3	42	106.7
3	76	7.6	22	55.9	43	109.2
3½	89	8.9	23	58.4	44	111.8
4	102	10.2	24	61.0	45	114.3
4½	114	11.4	25	63.5	46	116.8
5	127	12.7	25	66.0	47	119.4
6	152	15.2	27	68.6	48	121.9
7	178	17.8	28	71.1	49	124.5
8	203	20.3	29	73.7	50	127.0

About the Author

Anthony Guidice is a furnituremaker, teacher, and writer living in Rochester, New York. He is a contributing editor to *Woodwork Magazine* and conducts workshops and seminars on woodworking.